THE SEVEN DEADLY SINS TODAY

THE SEVEN DEADLY SINS TODAY

BY

HENRY FAIRLIE

DRAWINGS BY
VINT LAWRENCE

UNIVERSITY OF NOTRE DAME PRESS
NOTRE DAME   **LONDON**

Paperback edition published in 1979 by
University of Notre Dame Press
Notre Dame, Indiana 46556

Hardback edition published in 1978 by
New Republic Books
1220 Nineteenth Street, N.W.
Washington, D.C. 20036

Library of Congress Cataloging in Publication Data

Fairlie, Henry, 1924–
  The seven deadly sins today.

  Reprint of the ed. published by New Republic Books,
Washington.
  Bibliography: p.
  1. Deadly sins. I. Title.
[BV4626.F34 1979]   241'.3   79-893
ISBN 0-268-01698-4

Printed in the United States of America

CONTENTS

PREFACE
vii

THE FACT OF SIN
1

PRIDE OR SUPERBIA
37

ENVY OR INVIDIA
59

ANGER OR IRA
85

SLOTH OR ACEDIA
111

AVARICE OR AVARITIA
131

GLUTTONY OR GULA
153

LUST OR LUXURIA
173

THE PATHS OF LOVE
191

A CHECKLIST OF SOME BOOKS
215

This book is for
Betty and Bob
who have followed the paths of love
better than most.

PREFACE

AS OF NO other book that I have written, people have asked why I chose to write on the subject. The origin of the essays is clear in my own mind. I have for a long time thought that the psychological explanations of the way-wardness of our own behavior and the sociological explanations of the evils of our societies have come very nearly to a dead end. They have taken us so far, but not very far, and it is hard to see, in whatever direction they may move, that they will take us much farther. They have come to this impasse because they shirk the problem of evil, and they shirk it because of the major premise on which they rest: that our own faults and those of our societies are the result of some kind of mechanical failure, which has only to be diagnosed and understood for us to set it right. Yet none of the schemes for improvement, personal or social, have made much difference, and some would even say that they have made things worse.

There have especially been many tendencies in the modern age that have made us mischievously and in the end destructively egocentric, and even our societies are in danger of being left with no justification or function but to bolster our egotism. This was one of the themes in *The Spoiled Child of the Western World*—especially in the chapter "The Exhaustion of the Self"—and these essays continue that theme. They are addressed to the spoiled child that all of us are incited to become, and if the emphasis seems sometimes to be placed heavily on the young people of today, that is only because we can see in them the next stage in the decline into a listless self-concern. The behavior of the young reflects the attitudes of their elders.

This is not a work of theology, but its debt to theology is clear. Since the sins were defined by theology, we cannot and should not wish to escape from its definitions, even when we are unable wholly to accept them. I have consulted some theologians I know; the manuscript was shown to them. Although it would be too much to say that they have given the book their *imprimatur* and *nihil obstat,* they have been kind enough to say that its mere layman's grasp of theology at least does not offend in any important particular.

Some years ago the *Sunday Times* of London published a series on the Seven Deadly Sins, by seven of the best-known English writers of the day, which were then published as a book. I found them slender at the time and have still found them slender on rereading them, even though Angus Wilson on Envy and Christopher Sykes on Lust bear perusal. They nevertheless raise an interesting point. In his introduction to them, Raymond Mortimer says that although "in a series of articles such as I am introducing, passionate denunciations and threats of brimstone would be out of place, . . . the mildness with which on the whole they regard the deadly sins may be thought surprising and significant." In other words, they avoid moralizing, but at the cost of speaking very seriously about morality. I hope that I have avoided moralizing, but it is surely pointless to write of sin at all, if one is not prepared to speak strongly in moral terms.

Washington, D.C.   H.F.
Christmas 1977

THE FACT OF SIN

Peccatum poena peccati
Sin is the punishment of sin.

St. Augustine

THE FACT OF SIN

TO RAISE THE subject of sin is to provoke the interest and usually the humor of everyone; it is also to discover how limited is the range of humor on the subject. People seem compelled to try to be funny about sin, but the jokes are only variations on the theme that sin is fun, and of course that Lust especially is fun. There are some attempts at merriment about Gluttony, and to a lesser extent about Avarice and Sloth, but there the humor begins to falter. No one seems able to take Envy lightly, the thought of Anger is discomfiting, and that Pride is counted a sin causes mainly bewilderment. Everyone is responding differently to the "warm, disreputable" sins and to the "cold, respectable" ones.

But what is interesting is that when people are brought face to face with a sin, such as Envy, to which they are not willing to admit, they turn to look again at the sins, such as Lust, of which they were at first eager to boast. What has happened is that they have been made to confront the idea of sin itself—not of particular sins, lapses in our conduct that may not seem to count for much, but the fact of sin—and it is at this point that one realizes that, even in a secular age, we need to keep the idea of sin. Even the weakness of this statement, if left as it is, is characteristic of our own times. What it half-heartedly says is that, although we may not believe that sin exists, we nevertheless need to keep its shadow, just as we might say that, although we may not believe that God exists, we still need to keep his shadow. We must speak more directly. We sin.

We are not exempt from sinning simply because we do not believe that the willful violation of our humanity is no less a willful violation of our life in God; and even the most irreligious among us can have some idea of what that concept means. When a theologian says that "in each of the sins, a man acts in such a way as to make his relationship to God precarious, frightened, suspicion-laden, deceitful," it is not impossible for the irreligious to understand what he is saying, as they can also understand when he adds that "sin is what a man is compelled to confess to God because his action has placed him in a crisis before God." Certainly if one has no inkling of what he is talking about, one will understand why sin is more than moral evil, why it is commonly described as infidelity, why it has been said that sin is less like the act of a criminal than the act of a traitor. Betrayal and self-betrayal are in the substance of sin, and for the traitor there is rarely a way back. "As you have destroyed your life in this city," says Cavafy in a terrible line, "you have ruined it in the rest of the world."

One does not like to begin on so alarming a note. The prospect at once seems so desolate. One can almost hear the readers closing the book and turning quickly to panaceas that are less exacting. But if it seems so desolate, it can only be because the idea of sin, when we are forced to confront it, at once places its finger on something in ourselves of which we are aware, and of which we do not like to be reminded, when there are so many easier explanations to hand. If we fear what the idea of sin tells us of ourselves, it is because we fear ourselves.

Sin is the destruction of one's self as well as the destruction of one's relationships with others. But the fearfulness of the destruction cannot be grasped unless we realize that the damage is done precisely where each of our natures is organized by some unifying principle that is more than its parts, where there is something unknowable in us, which we nevertheless know to be most completely ourselves and with which we have each to form our own relationship:

> Below the surface stream, shallow and light,
> Of what we say we feel—below the stream,
> As light, of what we think we feel, there flows
> With noiseless current, strong, obscure and deep,
> The central stream of what we feel indeed.

This is where sin causes its devastation in us, at the very core of our beings, where life's flow is this noiseless, strong, deep, obscure current in us; and if to talk of God helps to reinforce our awareness of how deeply our personalities lie within us, and how severely we violate them when we sin, then the unbelieving may sometimes use His name without taking it in vain. At least we still vaguely understand it.

But in their secularization of everything else, the unbelieving must be careful not to secularize God. He is more than an Idea. He is more than the Word. He is more than Logos. There are too many unbelievers today—many of them even in our temples and churches—who take His name in vain. Perhaps no one sins more outrageously in our age, or is more characteristic of the slackness we tolerate, than the priest and the theologian who reduce God to no more than a concept but insist that they believe enough to remain members of their church or temple. They are making it awkward to be an atheist. Apparently one may now deny the teachings of Christianity—even a teaching as fundamental as the divinity of Christ, as some theologians have done at Oxford in the past year—and yet reserve the privilege of calling oneself a Christian. Why stand outside the doors of the church as an atheist, and think gravely of the falsehoods preached within that one feels compelled to combat, when all the time one could just step inside and in God's own house preach against them in His name? To deny that God is a Being and reduce Him to a mere concept, a figment of our making, a shadow of Himself, may leave one still a religious man in a trivial way, but it does not leave one a believing Jew or a believing Christian.

These essays are addressed to a secular age by someone who may best describe himself as a reluctant unbeliever. A Christian friend who read the first draft of them said that their accent was one of reverent disbelief. It is not a comfortable position to be in. Certainly it has few consolations. One lives with a hole in one's life, and the emptiness is ever-present, because one is so aware of it. Yet one cannot just fill it at one's wish and is certainly not willing to fill it with any flotsam that lies to hand, the wreckage of the beliefs in which one was raised, or of others to which one has leaned. There are those who are unable to believe, and are condemned eventually to hardly the most congenial circle of hell, while those who did not enjoy the opportunity to believe loll about in the relative ease and lack of discomfort of limbo. Perhaps one is among them, willful in one's refusal of grace, too proud to believe. But even if this is one's condition, one may still be allowed to say that it is important that we understand that we sin, and that we are able to say that we do. Lack of faith may itself, after all, be evidence of the sin of Sloth.

Sometimes even the unbeliever finds it difficult to talk in any but "religious" terms of that transcendent Other that all of us feel lies beyond the grasp of our everyday senses. We are not insensitive to what are conceived to be the divine attributes—infinity and eternity, omnipresence, omniscience, omnipotence, immutability, and unity—at work in creation and in ourselves. And when we attend to the deepest parts of our being, we find that our humanity can in the end only be defined, whether we like it or not, in terms of something that lies beyond it, and that is of deep significance to us.

When we read the views of today's agnostics or

atheists in a magazine such as the *Humanist*, their picture of human nature seems too dessicated and certainly too mechanical. We are reduced to things of pulleys and levers. Pull this one or that one, and this or that will happen. If many people are today attracted to feeble and unexacting forms of Eastern religions, if they talk trivially of mystical experiences that they pathetically imagine they have had, if astrology has returned as more than a jape in popular magazines and newspapers, it is partly because this shriveled concept of human nature has been found woefully inadequate. These follies are of course no improvement. They are a reaction. But the unbeliever who is modest has the need, and must even be allowed the right, to reach to the insights of his own civilization, not least of its theologies, to express what otherwise he is unable to utter or explain.

Although the sins are abundantly and vividly and, one may say, riotously described in the Old Testament, and although there are dire warnings against them in the New Testament, the idea of sin is preeminently a construction of Christian theology. One is immediately aware of this when one tries to describe any sin individually, searching for the point, to which one must always reach, at which it is clear that more than moral evil is being described. When one thinks of it, this is unavoidable. The definition of sin in Christian theology was part of its tremendous redefinition of human personality over the centuries. Since that redefinition, none other has taken us much further.

In the Middle Ages and even in what we used mistakenly to call the Dark Ages, our concept of human personality was continually expanded by the models, as we would now call them, with which Christian theology went about its work. It was a superb intellectual construction, but it was also a superb imaginative construction, as the vitality of its symbolism testifies in its art and literature. The idea of sin in general, and of the Seven Deadly Sins in particular, would not have taken so deep or strong a hold if they had not reflected a concept of human personality and its potentialities, both for good and for evil, that was being ceaselessly widened and deepened. In order to conceive the terrible destructiveness of sin, it was first necessary that our whole natures should have been conceived as so rich and intricate that there is something in them that can be terribly destroyed.

We have said that sin is more like the act of a traitor than the act of a criminal. In primitive societies the distinction was not really made. Sinning was the violation of tribal laws and customs. Attention was given to it as an outward act and not an inner inclination. Early societies were concerned mostly with the consequences of individual sins and did not yet have any notion of sin as such, something that lies within us, an ineradicable part of our human natures. We have only to turn to the Greek tragedies to recognize that, however profoundly they searched out human motives and confronted the facts of good and evil, there was something that in the end they did not explore. The evil of men in them is still law-defying. The evil men and women are criminals, who violate the laws of men and gods. But by the time we reach Shakespeare, sin is life-betraying. In his plays we are with traitors, who are unfaithful as well as disobedient. God has become more than his laws, as is of course most obvious in Dante, and although Shakespeare can hardly be described as a Christian writer, one thing that had intervened in the course of the centuries was the Christian vision of man, and it informed his own vision.

The Christian vision had built on another tradition, the story of the tribes of Israel. In the Old Testament the inner inclination to sin is already being explored. If sin is "what a man is compelled to confess to God," that voice is to be found throughout the Old Testament, as in the cry of the psalmist, "Against thee, and thee only, have I sinned," a confession that is made without the threat of divine punishment. It is the cry of a betrayer who repents his treachery. Joseph was thinking of neither divine nor human punishment when his master's wife entreated him to lie with her, and he replied that, since the pharoah had entrusted him with his household, and kept nothing from him except she who was his wife, how could he do such a great wickedness and sin against God? At this point, the trust he returns to his master and the trust he returns to God have become one and the same; sin is established as an act of infidelity and not only of disobedience, of a traitor and not only of a criminal.

In the *Oresteia*, when the oracle prescribes that Agamemnon should sacrifice his daughter Iphigenia, he does so, and the gods do not intervene to stop him. In the Old Testament, when God prescribes that Abraham should sacrifice his son Isaac, he prepares to do so, but God intervenes and stays his hands. Obedience to the divine will is strong in both stories, but in the Old Testament another factor has entered. To the justice of the gods is added the love of God, and the whole relationship of man with God is radically different. The gods had a destiny for Agamemnon, that he should be punished for the terrible crimes of the house of Atreus, and that destiny must be played out even at the cost of Iphigenia's life. But the destiny of Abraham is left open as the love of God works in him. His intuition of God's will is that Isaac should not be sacrificed, and the question of individual responsibility is at once raised to a different plane; raised with it is the question of sin.

There is still a great deal of legalism in the Old Testament idea of sin. The emphasis in the Sermon on the Mount is very different from that in the commandments that Moses brought down from Sinai. The commandments have been translated into beatitudes. "Blessed are the meek, for they shall inherit the earth," is not a sentence one could read in the Old Testament without a jolt, but by the time we reach it in the New Testament, we have been prepared for it. It is set in the context of the rest of Christ's life and teaching. Without that example the sentence carries little conviction, for there is no evidence that the meek do or ever will inherit the earth. We have been turned away from a concern merely with our outward acts, to contemplate what lies most deep in our innermost selves, hidden from all but ourselves and God; the corruption that is wrought there by our sinning; the disabling of our whole natures so that we diminish even our freedom as human beings; and the suppression in us—even the unbelievers among us—of all that we may reasonably call divine.

This is a tremendous expansion of our idea of human personality, and when we turn to the great doctors of the early church, we halt at words that are hardly to be found elsewhere. "Penitence is the mourning of man for the sin that he has done," says St. Ambrose, "and the resolve to do no more anything for which he ought to mourn." It is we that sorrow at our own sinning and, if we truly are repentant, our contrition "shall be heavy and grievous," says St. Bernard, "sharp and poignant in the heart." We do not sorrow at the punishment of God or men, but in ourselves that we have sinned. As St. Augustine said, in the words placed at the head of these essays, *Peccatum poena peccati,* "sin is the punishment of sin." There is no other formulation of the problem of human good and evil that so drives us back to our individual responsibility for our choices and to so vital an affirmation of our freedom as moral beings.

The classification of the Seven Deadly Sins had its origins in the monastic movement. "The list was first framed in the cloisters of the Eastern Church," and in the East it was and it "has always remained essentially a list of the vices besetting the monastic life." Even if that were all, we could not shrug them off. Perhaps one of the most unexpected facts about the pioneers of the monastic movements is the way in which many of them "plumbed the depths of the human heart in a way rarely equaled since." But perhaps we should expect it. If one is concerned to escape the temptations of the world, in order to devote one's life exclusively to the service and worship of God, one is likely to be acutely aware of what those temptations are and of our human frailty in face of them. Monks and nuns have a considerable amount of time in which to contemplate the ways of the world on which they have turned their backs, as well as the longings and temptations by which their flesh and spirit are still encumbered in the cloister and the cell.

One may say in passing that few things are more characteristic of our times than that the choice of monastic life is regarded as evidence of some kind of psychological disorder in those who take its vows. We all have to choose what parts of ourselves we will develop— we cannot be everything that we may be capable of being—but if some people choose to set aside their sexuality we think they are peculiar. Every popular movie about a nun's life makes it seem as if the novice who decides to leave the convent is healthy-minded, whereas the sisters whom she leaves behind are obviously women who have shriveled the most important part of their beings. Yet there is ample evidence, from their literature over the centuries, that those who have chosen the monastic life, men and women, are at least as fully developed as human beings, and suffer from as few or as many disorders, as those who have remained outside in the world.

Our unwillingness and inability to understand the monastic life extends even to the outside world. We have reached the stage of regarding a virgin as not quite healthy. She is certainly thought to be peculiar. Even some of the propaganda of Women's Liberation has, in its missionary emphasis on what it thinks of as sexual liberation, hardly been careful of preserving the reality of sexual choice, which must include the right to choose not to develop one's sexuality, no less if one is a man than if one is a woman. Why should men or women not decide, whether in a monastery or convent or not, that sexual activity is not the expression of their personalities in which they are most interested, or the pursuit to which they are most inclined to devote their lives? The flying nun may soon be thought to be one who performs the sexual act on a trapeze, and the vast contribution of the monastic movement to our civilization be neglected.

It was the ascetic, John Cassian of Marseilles, who introduced the rules of Eastern monasticism to the West, and with them the notion of the (eight) deadly sins. It was not the list as we know it today, but it was later modified by Gregory the Great, and it is Gregory's list that has prevailed. But the idea owes more to the great pope than that. He so defined the sins that they were "able to serve as a classification of the normal perils of the soul in the ordinary conditions of life," and not merely as a list of the temptations that those in the monastic life must resist. In the Middle Ages the perils of the sins were preached intensively, and in England at the end of the fourteenth century, Archbishop Peckham ordered every priest who had the cure of souls to expound "the Seven Deadly Sins and their branches" four times a year "in the vulgar tongue without any fantastical imagination or any manner [of] subtlety or curiosity."

We are fortunate to have such an exposition, eloquently rendered and yet "without fantastical imagination," in the "Parson's Tale" in the *Canterbury Tales* of Chaucer. Unlike some other representatives of the church in his tales, the Parson was a good and humble man, and Chaucer lets him give a straightforward sermon that is still compelling from start to finish. Its brilliance lies in the way in which the deadly sins are related to our day-to-day life. If it is the greatness of Dante that he lays bare our souls in his exposition of the sins, it is no less the greatness of Chaucer that he lays bare our conduct. Written about eight centuries after Gregory the Great, the "Parson's Tale" is far from being a monastic rule. We are asked to consider the extravagance of our clothing, the greediness of landlords, the richness of our food, the deceit of merchants, the raising of our children, the backbiting of gossips, and much more in the same vein— all of them examples from our ordinary behavior, no less relevant now than six hundred years ago. The vitality of the sermon lies in the fact that it is as forceful a demonstration as one could ask of the light that is thrown on our conduct by the concept of the Seven Deadly Sins. We might be listening with the pilgrims, but still we can find ourselves in his words.

Chaucer puts the sins in the same order as Gregory—to that we will come—but there is something at least as important as the order. The Seven Deadly Sins are "all leashed together," says the Parson; they are "the trunk of the tree from which others branch." This is the answer to those who ask, "Why these seven?" and not others of which they are acutely aware. For of course the others are included, the "branches" of the seven, and the more one explores the traditional classification, the more one finds that, not only is no other classification needed, but that none other will suffice as well. It is the interlocking that matters, the fact that the deadly sins are all leashed together, and it is this that is emphasized in the traditional classification. There are not simply all the individual sins we can count, of which we are guilty in one degree or another, there are these seven capital sins that lie deeply rooted in our natures. Faced by the descriptions of them, we know that we elude none. It becomes less easy for us to claim that, like the curate's egg, we are good in parts, guilty perhaps of Sin One, to some extent of Sin Four and Sin Six, and of course Sin Seven, but innocent of the rest and so, on balance, not all that bad a person after all. The cunning of this kind of self-absolution is obvious, and what we are forced to do, by the idea of the Seven Deadly Sins, is try to avoid this shallowness and instead to take responsibility for our whole natures and seek to know them in all their intricateness.

Cruelty, for example, is a sin. But if we think of it only as a sin on its own, it is comparatively easy for us to say that we are not often cruel. Not many of us are torturers, consciously and deliberately cruel to others, in temper or in practice. But if we realize that each of the Seven Deadly Sins can cause us to be cruel, we at once recognize that we are probably cruel more often than we think. We may admit to being avaricious or lustful—such admissions are easy enough to make from time to time—but how often do we stop to think that our Avarice or Lust—like all the rest of the capital sins—is likely to cause us to be cruel? When we look at it in this way, cruelty ceases to be an individual act, which may be explained if not excused by the circumstances; it becomes a deep inclination in us, something of which we are capable in many ways, that has its origins in these strong impulses of our natures.

It is being suggested on all sides today that, in a rather simple-minded way, we may just love each other as we are, without much being expected on either side. But the truth is that there is a great deal of emotional "ripping off"—licensed cruelty—in these easy-going relationships that is ignored. Someone is still likely to get hurt in them, however little may seem to have been asked, because it is difficult to prevent some human feeling from being aroused and so laid open to bruising and pain. People who expect and ask little of others will usually be found to expect and ask little of themselves. They will expect to have to give little, if to give anything at all. They will in particular not expect to have to correct any of the Pride, or Envy, or Anger, or Avarice, or Gluttony, or Sloth, or Lust, with which they are bound sometimes to hurt the other person. The excuses have been built in too easily: "I expect little of you, you expect little of me; I promise you nothing, you promise me nothing; so neither of us can hurt the other, or accuse the other of hurting." But if one gazes on such a relationship as it crumbles, as crumble it will, one usually sees that someone has been hurt, although he or she may fliply dismiss the pain to hide the weal across the face, as if the stricken heart may not cry its suffering aloud.

If we do not take seriously our capacity for evil, we are unable to take seriously our capacity for good. Both become little more than coincidences, the result of our genes and our psychology and our environment, for which our responsibility is unclear. Just as we can be little blamed for the evil we do, so we are as little entitled to take credit for the good. The concept of the Seven Deadly Sins has at least this to be said for it: that it does not allow us to compartmentalize our lives, any more than it lets us imagine that we can sin in compartments. It presents us each with the ultimate being that is wholly ourselves, beyond the influence of our genes and our psychology and our environment, for which ultimately and inescapably we are alone responsible. There is something enlivening in this, which reminds us that our lives, to a degree that counts, are always ours to make; that we may still choose to be more whole; that there is more and better in us, on which we can call, than we have so far chosen to become. The understanding that we sin is a summons to life.

It is characteristic of our age that people want to have God but do not want to have the Devil. People are inventing gods for themselves, with what I have elsewhere called their Do-It-Yourself God Kits. But they are gods who do not demand much of them, and they certainly are not gods who punish, although they are allowed to reward. On the contrary, their gods absolve them from conflict and doubt, massage them, pat them on the head, and, rather like their parents, tell them to run along, get stoned if they will, pick marigolds, and love. So easy it is to love! But above all they are gods who will not trouble them with the fact of evil. The problems of evil, suffering, and death are not confronted, but evaded and dismissed. The recipes are too easy. Twenty minutes of transcendental meditation, or of mindlessly chanting the name of god, or of simply standing on one's head,and the thing is done: One is again made whole, at peace with the world, with one's fellows, and of course with oneself. Universal harmony has never been offered so cheaply before.

Unfortunately, the Devil is cleverer than any guru. God may move in a mysterious way His wonders to perform, but the Devil moves in ingenious ones to accomplish his victories. He is rather like a hotel burglar, who goes down the corridor trying all the doors, until he finds one that is unlocked. "Resist the Devil," says the New Testament, "and he will flee you." Perhaps he will. But he is not easily locked out; he has too many passkeys. "The Devil is a gentleman," said Shelley, which is interesting as a comment on gentlemen but no less interesting about the Devil, because he often has the most civil manners and comes with impeccable letters of introduction. He was himself, after all, rather well-born, and, like the younger son of a good family who has fallen on bad times, he is very adept at insinuating himself into the best of company. His usual accent in literature, as in *The Screwtape Letters*, is one of exceptional civility; Screwtape in fact writes very much like a don at Magdalen.

"The Devil's cleverest wile is to convince us that he does not exist," said Baudelaire. This is not as difficult for him as one might suppose, since he is inside us already, and we do not care to look for him there. James Hogg wrote a long unknown, and still little known, novel in the eighteenth century, *The Confessions of a Justified*

Sinner, in which the hero (if he may be called that) encounters a stranger one day, who engages him in conversation and then became his fast friend. This friend materializes from nowhere, as when the two first met, and disappears as promptly and mysteriously. He leads the hero from corruption to corruption, until the final evil-doing and catastrophe, always with the justifications to hand that in the end make "the justified sinner" of the title. He is of course the Devil, encountered not outside the hero, but inside him, materializing when it is opportune, when the resistance to temptation is weakest. The story is full of illuminations, of which perhaps the most pleasing and instructive is the civility with which the Devil addresses the hero, as if gentleman was indeed speaking to gentleman. His address is irreproachable.

We can recognize evil in others, but if we wish to look on the face of sin, we will see it most clearly in ourselves. It cannot always be recognized or measured by its visible consequences. The face of Dorian Gray did not change where it could be seen; it changed only in the portrait in the attic of which only he knew. He could not hide his sin from himself. Sin is our secret from others. Only we know where, and how deeply, it has taken root in us. Although it is a universal presence in the world, although we know that others sin as well as ourselves, every discussion of it must proceed outward from ourselves. We learn more about the nature of sin from St. Augustine in his *Confessions* than in all the volumes of *The City of God*. The essays that follow are not confessions, although there are presumably some traces, not all of which one hopes are hypocritical, of one's own acquaintance with sin. They are written from the conviction that, as individuals and societies, we are trifling with the fact that sin exists, and that its power to destroy is as great as ever; from the belief that much of the fecklessness and triviality, dejection and faintheartedness, wasting and corruption, which we now feel around us, in our personal lives but also in our common lives, have their source exactly where we do not choose to look.

"If we say we have no sin," said St. John the Evangelist, "we deceive ourselves, and the truth is not in us." If we do not acknowledge its presence in us, we abandon such resistance as we might offer, even before the struggle has begun. We leave our door unlocked to the burglar. "An idle man is like a house that has no walls," says the Parson in his disquisition on Sloth; "the devils may enter on every side and shoot at him, he being thus unprotected, and tempt him on every side." This may be the particular evil of Sloth—as our mothers used to admonish us, Satan finds mischief for idle hands to do—but it is also more generally a danger. All too easily, if we do not understand the existence of sin in us, and not just our capacity for sometimes doing sinful things, we leave ourselves as houses without walls. We need to acknowledge that the inclination to sin is at the root of our natures.

If sin seems to us a strong and ominous word, as Karl Menninger puts it, it is worth realizing that, without the notion of it, our situation can seem even more ominous. If we do not acknowledge that the inclination to sin is part of our natures, then why has all our tinkering with ourselves and our societies over the centuries, all our sociologies and psychologies and psychoanalyses, reforms and experiments and therapies, not made our lives more virtuous and more happy than they are? Why do we have the feeling today that we may even be slipping back? If the vast accumulation of our knowledge and sheer ingenuity, our intelligence and energy, have achieved so little in the past, why do we imagine that they can achieve any more in the future? Why is it worth continuing the human endeavor, if we have no inclination to sin in us, and yet are unable to make our lives good and happy? What situation could be more ominous? There have of course been many minds in the modern age, once certain of the power of human knowledge to eradicate or at least lessen our capacity for evil-doing, that have ended only in disillusion and despair. *Mind at the End of Its Tether* was the last desolate cry of H.G. Wells, and he spoke in turn for both moods of our century—a too-facile hope on the one hand and, in reaction to it, a too-facile despair on the other—until it sometimes seems that we have no ground between that is not shifting and treacherous.

But if we acknowledge that our inclination to sin is part of our natures, and that we will never wholly eradicate it, there is at least something for us to do in our lives that will not in the end seem just futile and absurd, nothing but a willful gesture against the odds. We can try to make sense of evil and, in making sense of it, make sense of our lives, of what we attempt in them. We will not draw up preposterous schemes to make us all at once innocent, only to find that the flowery meadows of the earthly paradise do not spring up around us; neither will we pretend that our evil is the result of some maladjustment in our psychologies or our societies, only to find that when the next adjustment has been made we remain as evil as before. We will recognize that the inclination to evil is in our natures, that its existence in us presents us with moral choices, and that it is in making those choices that we form our characters. We may be given our natures, but we make our characters; and if it is in our natures to do evil, it can and ought to be in our characters to resist it. When we say that someone is a "good man" or "good woman," we do not mean that they are people from whom the inclination to evil is absent, but that they are people who have wrestled and still wrestle with it. We say that they are people of character, and rightly so, because they have formed their characters in the wrestling.

We can engage in the combat. We cannot count the victories. They are few, anyhow, and fragile. What is more, there are evil ways to resist evil, as when we succumb to self-righteousness, and they are not the easiest of tempters to resist. What counts is the quality of our endeavors. We can know our inclination to do evil, be alert to the subtlety of its stratagems, and contend with it in the right ways. So we form from our natures, which are largely the common condition of our humanity, the individual character that is our own unique creation, making of that character, for we can hardly hope to do more or attempt to do less, something that is more pleasing to others, and more rewarding to ourselves, than otherwise it might have been. If this is not meaning enough for a human life, if this endeavor is to be written off as an absurd gesture that we make between the cradle and the grave, then one wonders what can ever be meant by being human. To contend intricately with the evil that lies intricately in us, to do so in the right ways, and so each to make something of individual worth of the characters that we form—this is enough for a tombstone, even if not for beyond it, and it is also what has brightened, often enough for it to count, the long caravan of mankind across the centuries. We cannot afford to slight the notion that our resistence to our own evil, and the quality of our resistance, are themselves a purpose that makes our lives more than absurd, and that keeps us in touch with the divine.

If we acknowledge the existence of sin at all, we must acknowledge that there is original sin. But the idea of original sin, when it is popularized, and not least when it is secularized, is so abused that we need to be clear about it. One need not follow all of St. Augustine's interpretations of the Fall in order to recognize how searching is his insistence that our "first parents" were already wicked in themselves before they succumbed to the actual temptation, otherwise "the Devil would not have begun by an open and obvious sin to tempt man into doing something which God had forbidden." Man had already begun to seek satisfaction in himself and, consequently, to take pleasure in the words of the serpent: "Ye shall be as gods." We have said something of the same in secular terms: that the evil that we do, and the consequences of it which we can see, are not in themselves our sin, but have been preceded by it. If it helps to make the point, we may even make a verbal distinction: between our sin and our sinning. We may say that our sin is that we are in the frame of mind to listen to the Devil, before we do what he asks of us, while our sinning is that, having listened to him, we do not then resist and so do what he has asked.

The notion that every infant is born sinful is too simple—a statement of flamboyant rhetoric that tells us little—and its simpleness brings it too close to what is most repellent in the Augustinian notion of "original guilt." As St. Augustine said in a famous passage, "We are all in that one man [Adam], since we all were that one man who fell into sin"; our propagation is therefore "vitiated by sin," and we are "bound by the chain of death, and justly condemned." The sheer injustice of this—that original sin should imply our personal guilt before God and make us justly damned by Him, even before we have committed any act of our own—is irreconcilable with any notion of God's love, and is the kind of perversity that gives St. Augustine a bad name.

The idea of original sin is an attempt to account for the universal presence of sin in the world, in all human beings in every age in every culture. The result of the Fall was a loss of sanctifying grace, and the likelihood of our sinning. We are estranged from God. We are unable to know His will perfectly, and such of it as we can apprehend we cannot carry out completely. It is a tendency to sinfulness that is inherent in man, and these words—"inclination" and "tendency"—are crucial. They help to demystify the idea of sin, when its secularizers seem bent on mystifying it. Even if we do not share the belief that baptism remits original sin, we can nevertheless understand that, although it leaves us still subject to human disabilities, moral and physical, our free will remains. We may still choose a righteous course or a sinful one, to a degree that counts and in fact makes our lives human. We sin necessarily but willingly, says St. Augustine, in one of those stern and searching apothegms that reach across the centuries. "No one sins because God foresaw he would sin. No one sins unless it is his choice to sin; and his choice not to sin, that also God foresaw." His foreknowledge leaves us still free and therefore moral agents, and although the idea of original sin has been used to justify the various concepts of predestination, Catholic doctrine at least has never fully accepted them, and they need not concern us.

Let us try further to demystify the idea. We cannot at every moment in our lives, and in every occasion that we encounter, consider what we ought to do; we have sometimes to act by habit or out of what we may call intuition. Even when we do have the time and inclination to consider, we find that often we are not sure what we ought to do; the choices are difficult, and there seems to be much to be said on many sides. But even when we have determined what we think we ought to do, we often then fall far short of doing it; we are lazy in our performance, or we get distracted by something else, or we simply cannot summon the will to carry something through. None of this excuses us from trying, both to determine what we ought to do, what is morally demanded of us, whether by ourselves or by God or by some absolute moral standard that we acknowledge, and to do it to the best of our powers. We may not do all that is demanded—even all that we know is demanded—and we may not do exactly what is demanded. But we can do something in response; and to the extent that we try to do it, and then manage to do it, we are moral and free agents, able to choose a (somewhat more) righteous and (somewhat more) acceptable course, even though we will also still necessarily and willingly sin.

We must not be frightened of the idea of original sin. Let us say that it is in the natures of schoolchildren to be lazy and disobedient, that to be lazy and disobedient are "original sins" of schoolchildren—a fact that would seem to have been demonstrated by empirical evidence over the generations and that is confirmed by one's own memories of one's own schooldays. Then we will expect all schoolchildren to skimp their homework from time to time and to defy willfully the reasonable orders of their schoolteachers. This is their "original sin," for which they should be punished but not severely, because such lapses are to be expected. In a sense these lapses are not their fault, and we are not ascribing "original guilt" to them. In fact, we are suspicious of schoolchildren who are never lazy and never disobedient and think with some justification that there is something wrong with their natures. But if the lapses are more than occasional, if the schoolchildren *never* do their homework, and *always* defy the authority of their teachers, we are no longer dealing with their "original sin" as schoolchildren, but with an individual sinfulness that ought to carry with it an individual guilt, for which they ought to be appropriately and even severely punished. There are theories of child-rearing to which such an idea is abhorrent, but by most schoolteachers and parents and even most schoolchildren the distinction is understood.

It is much the same with the original sin that lies in us. Our lapses cannot be overlooked—the fact that we sin necessarily and willingly—but neither can we be too oppressed by them. If we are too oppressed by them, it is too easy to decide that there is no health in us, that there is no point in trying to do better, until we pass imperceptibly from the lapses, step by step, to embracing a life of sin, which we have in fact justified. This is particularly the sin of Sloth. In every account of sin in our literature, this step-by-step progression is noted. The sin is not jusitified by saying that it is right but by saying that one is helpless *not* to sin. There are in fact many children who, because their lapses were overlooked and no correction was applied, have then become oppressed by them and decided that they were helpless not to sin. The idea of original sin takes account of our lapses, and helps to explain them, but then still asks that we should find, as human beings who have our free wills, some response to the moral demands made on us, which if not perfect will at least be adequate. It is hard to see what is ominous in that—it could not be more human—and it is a tragedy that the concept has so often been distorted.

A moral demand must be a possible demand, one to which it is possible for those on whom it is made to respond adequately, and we come here to one of the most important considerations that will run through these essays, the relationship of the individual to his or her society. We are not born out of a vacuum, or into one, and we do not live in a vacuum. Our environment and our societies can make it more difficult for us to meet the moral demands that are made on us. They can make it less likely that we choose right and more likely that we will do sinful things. "A perfect life can only be lived in a perfect society," it has been said. "That is the difficulty of the Sermon on the Mount." (It is not its only diffficulty, one should perhaps add, before one feels too quickly exonerated.) Our sense of the individual responsibility that our inclination to sin imposes on us is so important that we must be careful not to seek any easy exoneration in the actual or supposed condition of our societies. But it is no less true that, to the extent that they make it more difficult for us to choose rightly, they cannot be easily excused either.

Sin is "whatever I do that mars, mauls, inflates,

depresses, distorts, or abandons" our humanity, and it can hardly be denied that our societies, as distinct from us as individuals, are capable of doing all these things. A book was published recently with the title *Sinful Social Structures*, and we need sometimes to think of our societies as sinning. The toleration of avoidable poverty is sinful. It is the sin of Avarice. The glut of foods and goods that we consume is sinful. It is the sin of Gluttony. The exploitation of sex is sinful. It is the sin of Lust. These are partly our own sinning—we are avaricious and gluttonous and lustful—but they are not entirely or only so. A society is not only the individuals who compose it. It has its own life, in its laws and institutions, customs and values, and through them it is able to impose on us. It can incite us to do what we ought not to do, and lull us into not doing what we ought to do. We may be ultimately responsible as individuals, since we could change our societies if we wished, but that they are capable of sinning on their own, even in our name, without our direct participation or approval, is beyond any question. If we neglect the poor, it is not only because each of us is avaricious, not even only because those who manage the economy may be particularly avaricious, but because the economic system itself is founded on Avarice.

If the sins are deadly to us as individuals, they are no less deadly to our societies. The feebleness of our societies, the steady weakening of all social bonds, is in part a consequence of their own sinning. One cannot expect individuals to be attached to their societies and to accept wholeheartedly their social responsibilities, if these societies are themselves perceived to be sinful. Our societies are (in part) what we obey—customs, laws, conventions—even when our obedience does not have to be enforced. Much of our obedience can and should be willing. The pupil who acknowledges the authority of his teacher's scholarship will be obedient to his teacher's authority in other respects, believing that it will be for his own good, even if he cannot see the point of some exercise that the teacher has imposed. He may also simply believe that his teacher deserves to be respected. If a society is to hold together for long, its members must have a similar respect for its authority, and so obey it willingly and not merely under the threat of punishment. But if a society is generally believed to be and to do evil, it cannot hope to kindle such allegiance, and its population will cease to be a citizenry.

The relationship of the individual to his society has seldom been less harmonious than now. The individual should find an inner personal satisfaction in the performance of his social responsibilities. But he hardly finds it today. Equally the society should be able to draw confidently on the spirited participation of all its members in its multifarious endeavors. But it can hardly do so now. The individual uses his society, and society uses the individual: That is today the breadth and depth of the relationship. It is a mutual bargain, not a joint enterprise; and even in the bargain, there is little exchange of trust. It is hard to think of a time in Western civilization when the individual has been so subject to society, yet felt so little attached to it; or when society has been forced to govern so much, but with so little authority to govern at all. The dislocation is so severe that it should tell us that we do not face only a few social problems, which we may meet with yet more feats of social engineering, but are confronted with a breakdown of all sense of mutuality, and not least of any shared understanding of what is meant by "ought," of the obligations that are attached to the rights that are bestowed and protected.

When it is secularized and applied to our relationships with our societies, the idea of original sin is most often used by conservatives. Since we are inherently so wicked, they say in effect, we cannot be trusted with the degree of freedom, least of all the equality of condition in which we might all enjoy this freedom, that we demand so imperiously. This has from the beginning, is now, and ever shall be, the political theology of the *National Review*, and of course of other conservatives; and what they are doing for secular purposes is once again to transform the idea of original sin into one of original guilt. If man is as inherently doomed to do evil as they say, there is little that society can do but truss him up. The notion that society is a partnership of its members, which will not confine them so much as free them to choose rightly, is not one that the conservative now entertains. There has to be only one backsliding, and he wags his finger and admonishes, "There is the old Adam in man."

To say that our natures are inclined to do evil is very different from saying that we are doomed to do evil. The first is a doctrine of hope and choice, the second a doctrine of despair and abdication. The conservative likes to think of himself as the most faithful of the guardians of society, yet he in fact leaves very little for society to do, very few ways in which it and its members can engage continually and fruitfully in a partnership. The laws and customs of society are to him little more than a moat, thrown round the keep in which those who govern it huddle fearfully, while everyone else is kept outside at a safe distance. The conservative today complains that our societies have no moral warrant. But it is he who reduces the grounds for their moral activity to little more than the suspicion that their citizens are untrustworthy.

It is not the function of essays such as these to prescribe what our societies should be like; or rather they may hint what they should be like, but it is not their function to propose the political or economic structure that seems most likely to achieve that end. "The New Testament, without going into details," says C.S. Lewis, "gives a pretty clear hint of what a fully Christian society would be like." He then says: "If there were such a society in existence and you or I visited it, I think we should come away with a curious impression. We should feel that its economic life was very socialistic and, in that sense 'advanced,' but that its family life and code of manner were rather old-fashioned, perhaps even ceremonious and aristocratic." Far from being provocative or paradoxical, these statements come near to a position that is very understandable. There is no reason why a society that is what we call "progressive" in its economic structure should also be what we call "progressive" in its cultural attitudes, why someone who believes in a more equal distribution of goods should also believe in more permissive standards of behavior.

There may have been a short period when this seemed to be so, when it seemed that every institution and symbol of authority was so interwoven with every other, that they all had to be called into question. But in fact those who wish to create an economically more just society—which demands a considerable measure of self-discipline in its members, if an external discipline is not to be imposed with unacceptable severity from the top—cannot welcome the weakening of social bonds that has been the mark of the modern age. Indeed much of what we call "permissiveness" in our societies today is only an extreme form of the very individualism that they wish to combat in the economic realm. There is a dilemma here for both the conservative and the socialist—to use the labels only as shorthand. The conservative wants to encourage individualism in the economic realm but to maintain the authority of institutions and conventions elsewhere in society; the socialist wishes to subdue individualism in the economic realm but again and again finds himself in alliance with those who claim for it in an absolute form in the rest of our lives. As for the liberal, he wavers between the two positions, managing to extract the worst from both of them, which is as much the reason as any, since his "philosophy" has governed our societies for so long, why they are today so weak and purposeless.

Until one or another of them establishes some coherent view that can be applied to the whole society, the relationship of the individual to his society, and of society to the individual, is bound to remain as unharmonious and meaningless as it is today. It is one of the convictions in these essays that, by speaking of our problems in the direct manner that is required when we speak of sinning, it is easier to see where the geological faults in our societies lie. The fundamental question that we should ask of our societies is whether they assist and encourage us to be good; the fundamental question that we should ask of ourselves is whether we wish to be good and encouraged and assisted by our societies to be so. This formulation is simple and old-fashioned; it does not by itself get us very far. But it is interesting, as perhaps these essays will show, how the political issues that we face, questions about our economies and societies, come newly alive when posed in terms of virtue.

We cannot say that sin is confined to the individual. We are to a large extent formed by our societies, and even the most nonconformist among us reflect our social environment and the times in which we live. But we must never stray far from the awareness that it is ultimately always as individuals that we sin, that it is at last alone that we choose to act either that much better or that much worse than we otherwise might. There is in these essays an implicit—at times, an explicit—criticism of psychiatry, of the excuses that it finds for us, and of the shallowness of the adjustments and accomodations that it invites us to make. Its explanations are our substitutes for the idea of sin, and in nothing is this more obvious than in the mirthlessness with which it encourages us to be interested in our lesser disorders, while it frees us from the dark night of the soul in which we must wrestle with our evil.

With a solemnity that can be justified only by the fees

that it extracts, our psychiatry points to the levers and pulleys that we may pull and push inside us, and by these simple exercises make our lives happier and more rewarding. (It is not much interested in whether they can be made more virtuous.) Only an age that does not know how to laugh could take such slight prescriptions so seriously. At least if we recognize that we sin, know that we are individually at war, we may go to war as warriors do, with something of valor and zest and even of mirth, for these are usually the most inseparable of companions. But to be told that in our disorders we are only responding to some disturbance in our lives just as others do, that there is a mechanical explanation of our woes that calls for no more than a mechanical reordering of our psyches—this calls for no valor or zest or mirth from us, and these are certainly the last qualities that we associate with our tedious little therapies. *Pilgrim's Progress* is a work of high adventure; one can hardly say that of psychoanalytical case histories.

As a result of the habits that psychiatry has encouraged in us, endlessly we scrape over our faults and weaknesses, which we ought to be able to take in good part in others and in ourselves, because we will not acknowledge that the real danger lies elsewhere and deeper. In no other age can people have been so apparently frank and serious about their peccadilloes, and so ready to confess them and publicly flagellate themselves for them at cocktail parties and dinner tables, but always to use these admissions of their disorders as a justification for not then resisting the total despoilation of sin, as if by some miracle of absolution what has been shown to be part of their natures need not then be combated. Mirthlessly and with self-importance, we confess to offenses that we know will be forgiven in order to justify the sin to which we are about to concede; so we give game, set, and match to the Devil, when he has won only an advantage. He finds a chink in our armor, where we have been found weak or at fault, and when he cries, "Aha! You are already lost!" we lay ourselves open to his much greater depredations.

Psychiatry is concerned with our natures, to make the distinction that has been suggested, and not with our characters. It is concerned with the raw materials among which we must sift in ourselves as we make our moral choices, and not with the actual act of moral choice and the kind of effort it asks of us. It therefore leaves us obsessed and intrigued by the raw materials of our natures, but casual and even frivolous in our attention to the kind of moral demands that we must make on them. "One of the Devil's most effective tricks to waylay us is to pick a fight with us," Kafka remarked. "It is like a fight with a woman which ends in bed." He makes us quarrelsome, and the quarrel only reinforces our sense of familiarity with him; he is full of innuendoes, that he knows us and what we are up to, until at last the fight seems pointless and wearying, and we decide that it is futile for us to carry it on or resist any longer. We are ready to concede, because he has robbed us of our perspective, even about ourselves. This is exactly the effect of the habits that psychiatry has encouraged in us. We are put into a state of constant quarrel with and between all the disorders and disturbances in our chaotic raw natures, until at the end of the day we are so wearied and even bored with ourselves that there is no real fight that we will wage.

What it can bring us to—all that these essays are intended to resist—all that is meant by sin—has been summarized by Shirley MacLaine. In an interview with the *Washington Post* in 1977, she said that "the most pleasurable journey you take is through yourself . . . that the only sustaining love involvement is with yourself." One gulps and reads on: "When you look back on your life and try to figure out where you've been and where you are going, when you look at your work, your love affairs, your marriages, your children, your pain, your happiness—when you examine all that closely, what you really find out is that the only person you really go to bed with is yourself. The only person you really dress is yourself. The only thing you have is working to the consummation of your own identity. And that's what I've been trying to do all my life. People always want to know where my drive comes from. Well, all I can say is my drive is what I have to do."

This is not only self-centeredness raised to self-obsession, but a rationalization for self-aggrandizement. There is in it not a hint of understanding or wishing to understand—of contrition or sadness—that a human spirit has become so vengefully uncaring of anyone or anything other than itself. Other people or other things that one's own life touches are merely extensions of oneself. So one goes to bed with oneself, a glacier in one's bed, as W.H. Auden once put it. For there is no understanding either that what is being described is a life that at its core has been reduced to ruins, among which all that can henceforth be enacted is a deathly masquerade. But also in it all and perhaps responsible to some extent for it all, there is again an appalling mirthlessness that must always accompany such self-absorption; in spite of the apparent boldness of the affirmation, there in fact is only a whimpering self-pity. Yet this is only one of many such documents we have today.

The search for one's "identity" has become so aggravating in our age precisely because the self has been reduced to this pinpoint of self-intimacy, and the bother about one's own self-in-itself is that it is very like everyone's self-in-itself. One tries to grasp the individual life in the words just quoted, but it at once crumbles in one's hand like a fortune cookie, and the fortune that is foretold in them is just as banal as that in the cookie. One cannot ask anything interesting about such a life, whether it has been good or bad, because the only standard by which it is lived is the drive to do "what I have to do." A life that is self-justifying is one that is uninteresting, because there are no questions one can put from one's own experience, or from the whole human experience over the centuries, to which the answer will not be given that "I did what I had to do." One is here at the lowest common denominator that an existence can reach.

Arguing against the kinds of psychiatry that do away with the categories of "good" and bad," and saying that he has met a "remarkable number of bad boys," William Gaylin, professor of clinical psychiatry at Columbia, has said recently: "Spare me, therefore, your good intentions, your inner sensitivities, your unarticulated and unexpressed love. And spare me also those tedious psychohistories which—by exposing the goodness inside the bad man, and the evil in the good—invariably establish a vulgar and perverse egalitarianism, as if the arrangement of what is outside and what is inside makes no difference." But it is exactly an example of this vulgar egalitarianism that we have just been noticing. One of the rewards of knowing and seeing that we can be evil, of acknowledging that individually we sin, and caring whether we do, is that we stand on our own feet on ground we choose and not in a common rut, unique as persons who never were before and never will be again and not merely as common denominators of a psychological or even the human condition, pusillanimous and faint-hearted, with no real taste of what freedom means. It was an English medieval philosopher who spoke of *hilaritas libertatis*, which may be freely translated as "the alive and delighting enjoyment of freedom," and one is left wondering if anyone but a Christian could have said it.

A word about the order in which the Seven Deadly Sins are discussed here. The order established by Gregory the Great, maintained throughout the Middle Ages, and followed by both Dante and Chaucer, has great power to it, and it is the order followed in these essays: Pride, Envy, Anger, Sloth, Avarice, Gluttony, Lust. There has been a tendency in modern times to advance Lust in the order, which could be said to reveal an obsession with sex, and to alter the placing of some of the others. In his work on *Moral and Pastoral Theology*, Henry Davis, a Jesuit, discusses the sins in this order: Pride, Avarice, Lust, Anger, Gluttony, Envy, Sloth; and the same order is followed in a contemporary handbook of moral theology, except that Envy and Anger change places. Both these volumes carry the appropriate *nihil obstat* and *imprimatur*, official declarations that they are free of doctrinal and moral error, and it would be absurd if it were regarded as either a doctrinal or moral offense to rearrange the order at one's own choosing. But it should not be at one's own whim, because the traditional order in which the sins are placed has a real significance, which is not that of suggesting that one is worse than another.

We are dealing with an elaborate intellectual construction that is intended to illustrate profound moral truths. All the Seven Deadly Sins are demonstrations of love that has gone wrong. They spring from the impulse, which is natural in man, to love what pleases him, but the love is misplaced or weakened or distorted. (It is characteristic of the intricacy of Christian theology that it should find the cause of sin in the same impulse to love that is also the root of all virtue.) Pride and Envy and Anger are sins of *perverted love*. The love is directed to a worthy object—in each case, to oneself—but it is directed in a false manner. The fault in them is that one imagines that one may gain some good for oneself by causing harm to others. Sloth is placed next as a sin of *defective love*. The love may be directed to a deserving object, but it is not given in a proper measure. Avarice and Gluttony and Lust are sins of *excessive love*. The love may again be directed to what in themselves are deserving objects, but it is so excessive that it interrupts, and must in the end destroy, one's capacity to love other objects that are also and perhaps even more deserving.

The first three sins are a rejection of community with others, evil forms of egotism, and are sometimes said to be the "cold" sins; the last three involve at least some community with others, however it is then perverted, and are sometimes said to be the "warm" sins. The "warm" should not be placed above the "cold," as long as it is understood that their placing in no way diminishes the devastation that they cause to oneself and to others. Because our societies are so abundant in material goods, and provide so many opportunities for physical gratification, we need to be reminded that these more physical sins can devour us spiritually. But at the top must still stand the sins of cold egotism. There is surely a considerable value in retaining this construction. It forces us to make differentiations with which we might otherwise not bother and to look more deeply for the roots of some evil act and at least to know where the trouble lies. If the sins begin in love, they end in lovelessness. Given that they are all loveless, they are all as serious. What the construction of the Seven Deadly Sins shows us is how various are the forms that this lovelessness can and does take.

The wisest observers of the passing scene have always remarked that, if one wishes to love the human race, one should not make the mistake of expecting too much of it. There is a wealth of common sense and humanity in that, and perhaps the most unexpected element in the idea of the Seven Deadly Sins is that, although it points with deadly accuracy to our capacity for evil, it also leaves us with a vivid and strong sense of what it means to be human. It picks its way so intricately among all the motives and passions by which we are moved, that it gives us at least the reassurance that it is very interesting to be human. But it is interesting only if we recognize that our natures are moral natures and that it is only when we sharpen our moral sense that we give them full play. "Morality like art," said G.K. Chesterton, "consists of drawing a line somewhere." We live in an age in which no lines seem to be drawn at all, and it is for this reason that our humanity seems a palsied thing of little reward to us. If we begin to take our sinning seriously, we might at least find that we can be interesting again.

CHAPTER ONE
PRIDE OR SUPERBIA

PRIDE OR SUPERBIA

PRIDE IS THE first of the sins, the root of the "bad will" of Adam and Even, the beginning of all sin, it is said in Ecclesiastes. Yet people are today often bewildered that it is counted as a sin at all. They ask: Should we not be proud of ourselves?

We say of someone who is sloppy in his appearance or careless in his work that he "takes no pride" in them. In other words, we criticize him for lack of pride. We also criticize those who, by their behavior to others, "leave them no pride." There is pride in the statement, "Black is beautiful," and surely it is right to be so proud. All of which is true. When the word is used in this way, pride is a justifiable sense of one's own worth. It is self-esteem and self-respect, as long as these are fitting. Its consequences may be good. We may be prompted by such pride to try not to fall below our own standards, to do better than before, even to attempt the best of which we are capable. How can this pride be regarded as sinful?

But a reasonable and justified self-esteem is not what is meant by the sin of Pride. The first definition of pride in the dictionaries is of something unfitting. "An inordinate self-esteem," says *Webster's*, as also does the *Oxford English Dictionary:* "an unreasonable conceit of superiority . . . an overweening opinion of one's own qualities." Its synonyms or near-synonyms are not attractive: vanity, vainglory, conceit, arrogance, egotism, boastfulness, self-glorification, selfishness, and many more, all of which we use as terms of reproach. There is some cunning in the question, "Should we not be proud of ourselves?" Even as it is so innocently put, there is already a note of vanity and self-satisfaction in it, and one feels that the Devil is there, alert as ever, making an opening for the real sin of Pride to enter.

"Being proud of oneself" is often equated today with "feeling good about oneself"; and feeling good about oneself is an altogether laudable ambition, but again only as long as one has adequate reasons for feeling good. As the phrase has sprung into popular speech in recent years, distilled from the reassuring little therapies of our time, it sometimes seems to be an all-embracing justification for being anything (or nothing). As long as one feels good about oneself, a multitude of sins are covered. But it is possible to feel good about oneself in states of total vacuity, euphoria, intoxication, and self-indulgence, and it is even possible when we are doing wrong and know what we are doing. "Should we not be proud of ourselves?" can invite far too easy a reassurance. If our self-esteem is to be justified, it needs more than "doing one's own thing," and feeling good about ourselves while we are doing it.

"Doing one's own thing," or any of the other similar passwords of our time, such as "I'm OK, you're OK," may seem to have little Pride in them. Where is the claim to superiority in them? Do they not merely ask to be allowed to live and let live? But what we eventually find in them is an assertion of self-sufficiency—a denial of one's *need for community* with others, which is in fact a form of selfishness, since it is always accompanied by a refusal of one's *obligation of community* with others. The steps from a reasonable self-concern to an utter selfishness are short and swift. Most of the prescriptions for "self-actualization" today are rationalizations for an aggressive self-centeredness and, in some of their forms, for violent aggression by one's self against other selves that get in the way. If it is not aggression, then it is manipulation, and the end is always the same: always striking or maneuvering to take first place, to domineer over other's and one's environment, even to seek revenge for real or supposed slights. What is invited is Pride.

If we are to claim that the self-love of pride is justified, it had better be in as strenuous terms as those used by Aristotle: "If anyone made it his constant endeavor to set an example in performing just or temperate or any other kind of virtuous actions, and in general always claimed the prerogative of acting honorably, certainly no one would reproach him with being a self-lover. . . . So it is right for the good man to be self-loving, because then he will both be benefited himself by performing fine actions, and also help others. But it is not right for the bad man, because he will injure himself and his neighbors by giving way to base feelings." It is right to be self-loving if one pursues what is morally fine, because the good man does what he ought to do; but it is not right "in the sense in which most people are self-loving," because what the bad man does is not usually what he ought to do. Few of our prescriptions for self-love today are concerned with the moral quality of our actions or use it as any measure at all; certainly they do not ask us to consider any more than a selfish purpose to our lives, for always its affirmations begin with "I - I - I."

Pride is camel-nosed, as Angus Wilson has said. It is also high-blown, puffed-up, stuck-up, stiff-necked. All of these are epithets, not only of superiority, but of aloofness. The proud man sets himself up and, in doing so, sets himself apart. A tower is one of the commonest metaphors of Pride. It is lofty and inaccessible. When we say that someone towers over us—as a parent may over a child—we are talking of someone who cannot be reached. We speak of an ivory tower as a place of self-willed retreat from the world, and there is Pride in that also. When it is proud, "the soul becomes inordinately pleased with itself," and it makes a solitary world, self-sufficient, walled in by its self-pleasing. If all the sins are causes of solitariness, Pride is the first begetter of it. "To be in oneself in the sense of to please oneself," says St. Augustine, "is not to be wholly nothing but to be approaching nothingness." There is today evidence of this all around us, in the vacancy of lives that are lived only for themselves.

When Dante encounters the proud in purgatory, they are each carrying the crushing weight of a huge stone, which bends them double, so that they cannot lift their eyes from the ground. Those who looked down on everyone else in their lives are now unable to look up at anything. "Alas, proud Christians," he exclaims. Seen as they are, their Pride avails them nothing. There is a sense in which this has already been their condition on earth. (Those who look down all the time, says C.S. Lewis, will not look up to find God.) The proud may look down on everyone else, but from their lofty gaze, from the tower where they have set themselves up, they in fact can see little. Stiff-necked they look down their camel-noses and can hardly see those at their feet. They are beneath their notice, as the saying goes. A lordly man will say that his townhouse is empty for the summer, even though it is still full of servants. He simply does not see the servants as people; in fact he does not see them at all. In all the metaphors we have for pride—as when we say that someone gets on his high horse—there is always this element of withdrawal from others. One is satisfied with oneself; only oneself is necessary.

Pride is the cause of disobedience, which sets one willfully at odds with lawful authority, in the family or in society. Pride is the cause of boasting and hypocrisy, which make it impossible to communicate intelligently with others. Pride is the cause of scorn and presumption and arrogance, which erect barriers against those with whom one comes in contact. Pride is the cause of impatience and obstinacy, which lead to strife rather than cooperation with other people. Pride is the cause of self-centeredness and vainglory, which set one apart to do merely as one wishes. Pride leads to such a swelling of the heart, filled with its own self-pleasure, that there is no place for others in it. The opposite of these consequences of Pride is of course to be found in Paul's famous words to the Corinthians about love, to which the King James Version gives the name of charity: "Charity suffereth long, and is kind; charity envieth not; charity vaunteth not itself, is not puffed up, Doth not behave itself unseemly, seeketh not her own, is not easily provoked, thinketh no evil; Rejoiceth not in iniquity, but rejoiceth in the truth; Beareth all things, believeth all things, hopeth all things, endureth all things. Charity never faileth." If we think that it is only the rich and the powerful who can be proud, we should pause to consider how little our actions each day reflect the words of Paul and how much the evils of Pride.

We will encounter all of these evils in various forms in the other sins. But it is only when we know the working of Pride in us that we see how deeply the sins are interwoven. Here is the keystone of the arch, and once we recognize that it runs through almost everything that we do, everywhere in our natures, we are in a better position to fight the other sins. This is the importance of the warning of Dorothy Sayers, that "the devilish strategy of Pride is that it attacks us, not in our weakest points, but in our strongest. It is preeminently the sin of the noble mind." Not only of the noble, but also of the righteous. Self-righteousness is a common and peculiarly loathsome form of Pride. When we encounter it in the noble mind, Pride is like a taint or flaw. It suffuses the whole character of the person, even where that character is apparently noblest or strongest. If it lies so pervasively in the best, it must lie at least equally so in us.

Pride is in our Envy, persuading us that we deserve better than we have, even to be other than we are, and so inciting us to pull down whatever we perceive to be superior to us. Pride is in our Anger, in which we adopt a position of superiority from which our scorn and obstinacy, and even our elation, will not let us be budged. Pride is in our Avarice, prompting us to display ourselves in "an extravagant array of clothing," as the Parson puts it in Chaucer's tale, and in "keeping up great households," which we do not need. Pride is in our Gluttony, in the display again of an "excess of divers meats and drinks; and especially in "certain baked meats and made-dishes," as the Parson says with his usual spirit, "burning with spirituous liquors and decorated and castellated with paper, and in similar waste." (There goes the crepe suzette! And the crown of lamb!) Pride is in our Sloth, in our assurance that we may get by with a minimum of effort and find achievement and reward by sluggishness. Pride is in our Lust, in our scant regard for the flesh and feelings of others, and our belief that we may dehumanize them and ourselves and still be regarded as human. Pride is the sustainer of our sinning, the reinforcer of all its motives.

What one notices in these examples is the element of competitiveness. Pride must be competitive, since it cannot bear to concede first place to anyone else, even when its real wants are satisfied. There may be both Avarice and Envy in the relentless striving for status symbols, but behind them is the Pride that wishes to display its superiority. It is nothing but Pride that gives us pleasure in having more than our neighbors, and of course of making sure that it is known that we have more. This competitiveness must separate people from each other—again it is a source of solitariness—and at its worst it leads to enmity against anyone who challenges one's superiority. One becomes in one's Pride a hater and despiser of one's fellow men. As Omberto Aldobrandesco, one of the proud whom Dante meets in purgatory, exclaims aloud: "Ancient blood, past chivalry, / These puffed me up—for-

getting in my pride / The common mother of humanity—
To such contempt of all the world beside"; and Oderisi of
Umbria, the celebrated illuminator of manuscripts whom
Dante also meets, says in turn: "ardour to outshine/
Burned in my bosom with a kind of rage." Contempt for
all the world. . . . The rage to outshine. . . . Forgetting the
commonness of our birth. Always the emphasis is on the
separation from others, the refusal of community, the
hostility that then burns all the time inside one.

There will be many who think that they are exempt
from such passions. But the pleasure that we are today
incited to take in ourselves, not only isolates us from each
other; it separates a few minute aspects of our own
beings, to exalt them above the full richness of which we
are capable as human beings. Pride may excite us to take
too much pleasure in ourselves, but it does not encourage us to take pleasure in our humanity, in what is commonly shared by all of us as social beings. The turning in
to ourselves has turned us away from our societies. It is a
sin of neglect: It causes us to ignore others. It is a sin of
aggression: It provokes us to hurt others. It is a sin of con-
descension: It makes us patronize others. All of these are
turned against our neighbors, and often in our Pride we
do not realize how aloof we have become, and how cut off
even from what in our own nature we should most deeply
know and enjoy.

As William F. May says, this withdrawal may take
many forms: the intellectual who "retreats from the
mediocrities of mass culture into the inner community of
taste"; the liberal who "retreats from the moral failures of
those who are wielders of power into the inner community of criticism and virtue"; the reactionary who "retreats
into impossible dreams about a bygone past to escape
contact with and responsibility for the present"; the
academic who "retreats from the simplicities of the common life into the complexities of his expertise." But the
most widespread form that it takes today is simply the

retreat of people into their private lives. As long as their society provides them with a reasonable degree of personal security and affluence, and the necessary means and opportunities to entertain themselves, it may be left to function and be managed as may be, no matter that it is still an unfit place for others to live in. We at least have "made it," and having made it, need only to be left alone.

No one can read *Helter Skelter,* the best account that we have so far of Charles Manson and his "family," without looking severely at himself and at our societies. Most interesting and perhaps most haunting are the rationalizations that Manson used, and that his followers then parroted as they carried out his orders. They constantly used the phrase "the Establishment" as a self-justification—the members of "the Establishment" must die—and one of them in fact used the phrase to her victim as she committed the final atrocity on her. The idea of "the Establishment"—together with many other muddled ideas—was necessary to sustain their exaltation. They were the avengers of society against its enemies. They would decide who would or would not exist. Although it will be resisted by many, it needs to be said that there is a very thin line to be drawn, if a line at all, between them and the radical terrorists who keep forcing themselves on our attention, the children of an affluent middle-class that is demoralized in the most literal of senses. They are closer, in motive as well as method, than may seem at first.

Charles Manson and his followers did not murder from Anger: Many others at the time were entitled to such credit as anger may be allowed. They did not murder from Envy: They were strangely impersonal about their victims, their eyes were not fixed on them in resentment. They did not murder from Avarice: Theft was not their motive, they took nothing; and equally they did not murder from Gluttony. They did not murder from Sloth:

One feels a dejection of the spirit in them, but it was not this which they were fleeing. They did not murder from Lust: They did not interfere sexually with their victims, and their own sexual life in the "family" may have been tawdry, but it was hardly an overwhelming concern to them. They murdered in the self-exaltation of Pride and from the incitements to it in our time. They had been taught to be pleased in themselves, with whatever they felt they were, felt they felt, and so felt they must do. They had been released to act as gods, wholly free from any human limitations.

We must understand the root of Pride. More than any other of the sins we associate Pride with rebellion, and it is the sin most difficult to discuss without referring to the rebellion of "our first parents." They were already wicked in themselves, as we have seen, before they succumbed to the temptation; and by wicked in themselves, we mean exalted in themselves, until they were ready to invite destruction and the destruction of their world. *Ante ruinam exaltur*—"before destruction the heart of man is exalted." St. Augustine's words are stronger than the more common phrase: "Pride goeth before a fall." The exaltation does not just precede the downfall but is closely associated with it. We become rash and self-willed. We *can* do anything, so we *will* do anything, regardless of its consequences. We think we are as gods. These are the marks of rebelliousness, not least the rebelliousness of the child.

They are the marks also of the radical terrorists who now take such a license to be society's avengers; and it must to some extent be true of any societies that are founded on what today we abjectly call the youth culture. There are pathetic waifs all around us who have been zealously instructed in Pride from their cradle. Far from it being our object to subdue it in them, we have mindlessly excited it in them. We have confirmed in them the belief that there is already inside them a fully developed self, that they are equipped to know that self, and that armed with this self-knowledge they may do as they wish. To say of children and the young that "they are persons, too," is obviously true to some extent, although what is true about it is uninteresting and banal. But used as it is today, it is a recipe for freeing the child from all restraint, of encouraging Pride in it. It becomes too pleased with itself. It has been taught both to exalt its own personality and yet search that personality only shallowly.

From it comes the adult. We have only to look at ourselves to see what tedious and trivial chroniclers we have become of our selves and our lives. We exalt what is little more than a self-intriguing but idle curiosity about ourselves into the pretense that we are seriously engaged in trying to know ourselves. Any glimmering of what we feel—what we *think* we feel, or *feel* we feel, or *say* we feel—we count as a genuine form of self-knowledge. This knowledge is accessible, of course, only to each of us as individuals. It is thus set beyond any challenge by others, and may be used to claim the right to do what we want, in response to any whim or fancy of the moment. People often talk today of their "need" to express themselves in some choice of the moment—action, word, gesture—and this "need" is then presented as the only justification that is required for their whim. This is the morality of the child.

Pride is the most persistent of our sins. The urge to the others may wax and wane, but Pride is a fixture in our natures. It comes early, it has been said, and it stays late. It is there in us when we are young. Michael Oakeshott has talked of the "sweet solipsism" of youth, and this self-centeredness of the young is engaging in a way. It is natural that they should be interested in finding out who and what they are. The young have not yet encountered the boundaries of real life; they do not yet know that for everything a price has to be paid, that what we use to pay for one thing cannot then be used to pay for another. The young are hardly to be criticized for this condition—youth would not be youth without this sweet solipsism—but an adult society can be criticized for adulating them and even imitating their condition. Solipsism has the same characteristic as Pride: The self becomes "the center about which the will and desire revolve." That such a beguiling but natural condition in the young should be so confirmed and encouraged by our societies that it becomes the natural and beguiling condition of adulthood is evidence of the license that we have given to Pride.

Spinoza calls Pride a "species of madness, wherein a man dreams with his eyes open, thinking that he can accomplish all things that fall within the scope of his conception, and thereupon accounting them real, so long as he is unable to conceive anything which excludes their existence and determines his own power of action." It sometimes seems as if this madness is abroad as never before. We have given a license to every form of nihilism, which may seem to be the opposite of Pride, but is in fact an extreme form of it and can be a pleasurable one. It is not unpleasing, after all, to deny all existence, even to make existence seem senseless. In its more general forms, nihilism feeds our Pride. We may decide what is and is not good, what is and is not absurd, what does and does not exist, what deserves and does not deserve to live. It tells us that we are gods in this small moment in which we live. The kinds of debased nihilism that run through so many attitudes today are, like Pride itself, a denial of human limitations and the boundaries of real life.

The rebelliousness against these limits now runs deep in us, and without an awareness of our own Pride we will not learn what we have to learn from Manson's story, and will dismiss it as just another case of psychopathology. This is not to excuse him, or to say that we are like him, or that we would in any circumstances act as he did. But it is to say that beyond his sickness, which we do not share, there lies a sinfulness that we do share. Sin acted in Manson on a sick mind. That does not exempt us from the sin merely because our minds are healthier. Manson and those who did this bidding did not spring from a vacuum; they sprang from a time and place that are ours as well as theirs. The rebelliousness of the self against all that might constrain it has been given too loose a rein for too long. The opposite of Pride is humility, but when this is now mentioned, one finds that it is no longer held in very high regard. That we should be so uncomfortable at the thought of humility makes us realize just how unchecked our Pride now is by our societies.

There is an unshakable air of unreality in our turning in to ourselves and our private lives for all our satisfactions. Our gratification in them has an implausible quality of daydreaming, often accompanied by a more plausible quality of desperation. (We *are* pleased with ourselves! We *are* satisfied with our lives! Our protests are suspect.) We do not have to look far to find who incites this daydreaming in us. If our commercial societies know how strongly they may appeal to our Avarice, they know no less how to seek out our Pride. They would much rather that we be pleased with ourselves in our private lives, where we may indeed imagine that we are as gods, than that we be discontented with our societies and our relationships with them. So they divert us from any serious concern with what is other than us. In short, our societies appeal to the very sin in us that must destroy them, our self-love. It has been exalted as the motive by which our societies must be driven, whereas it is the motive that must ultimately undermine all social bonds.

There is no way in which the conservative of deeply moral impulse can pretend that these small-spirited societies of ours are the societies that he is bidden to defend. There is no way in which the liberal can pretend that he can any longer remain in an unquestioning and unholy alliance with a commercial system that appeals to no other motive than those of self-love and self-approval. There is no way even the socialist can hope to change those societies unless he appeals to a moral order beyond that which we and our societies have so single-mindedly entertained for so long. Pride is a sin of self-ishness—self-centeredness, self-satisfaction, self-exal-tation—and on selfishness our societies are founded. It is they that have stirred up the motive of self-love too per-sistently and for too long; they cannot then be surprised if it takes exotic and terrible forms. Equally we cannot be surprised that, when people begin to look for exotic and terrible forms of self-pleasing, our commercial societies are at once in the marketplace to supply them.

Our culture is not unaffected by the economic sys-tem. Seeing the individual set apart in his ivory tower. the private life that he enjoys as a member of the middle class, our culture in turn has assured him that there he may as an individual find happiness, at least such hap-piness as may with luck be attainable. Our art and literature both assist in the isolation of the individual. They describe what is supposed to be going on in our-selves, including our response to them, until that is all that interests us. The wider society in which we live is simp-ly absent from them. (After all, there is not much of the wider society to be shown in the bedroom, where so much of our literature and theater and cinema now hovers.) Personal relationships are cultivated at the ex-pense of all social relationships, but even these in the end bring only tedium and solitude, and the individual is then encouraged to retreat still further, from the tiny space that he has been cultivating around him, into a realm of "inner space" where he will find and need to cultivate only himself. When God asked Adam after he had sinned, "Where art thou?" it was not because God did not know, since he knows everything, but because he was scolding Adam, reminding him that "there really was nowhere he could go, once God was not in him." He was at last only in himself, there vainly to look for satisfaction. "Where art thou?" we may ask ourselves now, and we are nowhere, except in an inner emptiness of ourselves.

It is from this that so much of the rest of our sinning flows. If the proud man is approaching nothingness, St. Augustine could not have foreseen that we would so rush to embrace it. The curious thing about our self-absorption—curious only until one thinks about it—is that it seems to bring so little contentment. People have never been more agitated about themselves, wondering all the time whether they are "actualizing" their selves to the full. Their little efforts are called "self-improvement," but always a self-improvement, as it turns out, that is measured only by how good one feels about oneself. In bookstores there are sections that are devoted to "Sexuality and Self-improvement," and the placing of the two together tells how shallow is the exercise. People watch their moods and feelings now as they watch the bathroom scales and turn to new therapies in the same way as to new diets. But this search for self-pleasing brings no contentment. They are still agitated. There must be better. There must be more. This discontent is always one of the punishments of Pride, the consequence of the illusions of self-sufficiency that it encourages.

But there is a more profound cause for this aggravation. Human beings are moral beings. Our natures are moral natures. Morality is concerned with the rightness and wrongness of our actions, and our actions affect not only ourselves but other people. It has been said in theological terms, "A man does not meet God, much less evade God, in an encounter isolated from his world and neighbors"; and it may equally be said that, in an encounter isolated from others, he may succeed in evading himself, but will not meet himself. Morality is the choice between possible courses of action. If that choice revolves round only oneself, there is in fact no choice at all, but merely a submission to one or other whim or impulse. There is no real will of one's own to decide what one should do. "I can never find out what my own will is by merely brooding on my natural desires, or by following my momentary caprices," says Josiah Royce, and he reiterates, "Left to myself alone, I can never find out what my will is," because there is never just one desire present in us but a heap of conflicting desires. How can one decide what one ought to do, if the object is only one's self-pleasure, since so many things seem desirable at the same moment?

If we are ever to be as fully ourselves as we may be, a concern for others must be present in our choices. Duty or loyalty or conscience—call it what one will—must consistently be one of the governors of our actions. To strip people of their moral natures is in fact to strip them also of the possibility of fully being. Self-pleasing is the vanity of Pride, and it is the form that it most obviously takes today. The person who is vain is empty. "Vain describes what is absolutely lacking in value or worth," according to *Webster*'s, "or what is relatively insignificant or unavailing." If the self is turned in to only its self-pleasing, it is this worthlessness and insignificance that it will find. To punish him for his vanity, the gods made Narcissus fall in love with his reflection, and gazing at it he wasted away. He "does not fall in love with his reflection because it is beautiful, but because it is *his*," W.H. Auden said. "If it were his beauty that enthralled him, he would be set free in a few years by its fading." That he wasted away in his self-love is only a symbol of the wasting away of lives that we can see all around us today. They are lives that are vacant, in the pursuit of self-pleasure, as the expressions on their faces are vacant. Vacant of interest. Vacant of purpose. Vacant of experience. Vacant of commitment. Our societies are satisfied that they should be so, since in such a transfixed state they cause no trouble, and do not question where our societies are leading us.

Narcissus loved himself rather than the nymphs, and Auden even suggests that he loved himself for the satisfaction of not loving the nymphs. There is the same trap in the Pride of our own age, in which self-love is exalted above love for others. To imagine that one does not need community with others is a terrible form of Pride. The refusal by many people today of commitment in their personal lives is reflected in a similar refusal of commitment to the wider society. Human beings have a need for social existence, and by that one does not mean going to cocktail parties or to singles bars, both of which represent the opposite of social existence and are substitutes for it. The wish to be Jonathan Livingston Seagull a few years ago was a wish to be free of all such engagement, commitment, and involvement, to do what man cannot do, glide carefree on the wind and breeze, above and beyond the mundane life of his world. If it was thought that the flight of Jonathan Livingston Seagull, as one commentator said, "romantically symbolized the free spirit of the heroic individual," then it was the falsest kind of romanticism. It suited the time, the illusion that one can be free and heroic and strong in isolation, and perhaps only in isolation. It led quickly to disillusion, but not to the pulling up of the root, the false and exaggerated individualism of our age. The individual has merely turned further in to be unheroic.

Unheroic but still alone; alone and so still free. The freedom that is claimed is the freedom from responsibility, for anyone else or for the wider society, and with the freedom from responsibility goes the freedom from guilt. The supposed innocence of a few years ago has given way to a prevailing cynicism—the rip-off is now a proclaimed way of life—but what has been common to both moods has been the self-excusing from any feelings of guilt. In both cases, there is Pride. Whether one is claiming to be so innocent that the morality of one's actions is beyond any question, or so uninnocent that it is irrelevant to raise any questions about their morality at all, one is again setting oneself above and apart from society with no judge of one's actions but oneself. Our societies are content that their members should thus absolve themselves from responsibility and guilt, for, if such feelings were to overtake them, they might begin to concern themselves with how these societies are themselves organized and to what ends. A people absorbed in self-love will not be moved by love for their neighbors to inquire how their societies are caring for those less fortunate than themselves.

The self-love of Pride today is more unbridled than at any other time. Nothing is set against the individual, nourished to be presumptuous and vain, to command his duty or his loyalty, except the power of the state, a power that the individual then boasts of evading. Since the state is feared, and certainly is not loved, the individual is released still further, to do simply what he will. The society and culture in fact egg him on to more and greater acts of Pride, for as a self-pleasing individual he can easily be appeased by mere trifles. In reinforcing the distorted claims of the individual, our culture has both consciously and unconsciously done the bidding of commerce, and helped to destroy every institution that might have resisted it. If there is today no avant-garde feared by those in positions of power and influence, the reason is social and not aesthetic. In fact, it is political. There is nothing for them to fear from our art or our literature, which can be left to entertain the individual, while the commercial system satiates him. To keep us quiet, we are made trivial.

The working of Pride in us will be seen in the rest of the sins. But it is worth returning for a moment to the fact that humility is today looked upon with such scant regard that it is almost embarrassing to mention it. There is a common misunderstanding in this response. A false humility is no more to be praised than a false pride, depreciating oneself too much is as wrong as esteeming oneself too much. According to Aristotle in his table of virtues and vices, if "magnanimity" or a proper pride is the mean, and vanity is its excess, its deficiency is what he calls "pusillanimity." "The man who has too low an opinion of his own worth is pusillanimous, and it makes no difference whether his worth is great or moderate or little, if his opinion of it is too low." To be humble is not to "put oneself down," as the phrase is now understood. Humility is defined by St. Thomas Aquinas as "a praiseworthy depreciation of oneself to the very lowest degree," but the vital meaning here is that the self-depreciation will not be praiseworthy if it is false. One can also sin by thinking too little or too meanly of oneself.

As he leaves the proud in purgatory, the Angel of Humility comes to Dante, to lead him to the next cornice, and even in translation one catches the radiance of the moment:

> On came the beauteous creature, clothed in white,
>   And seeming as he came in countenance
>   A star of dawn all tremulous with light.

> He spread his arms abroad, and spread his vans,
>   And, "Come," said he, "the stairs are nigh; henceforth
>   An easier climb is yours and every man's."

As he leaves Pride behind him, "voices in our ear / Sang out *Beati pauperes spiritu*: No tongue could tell how sweet they were to hear." It is the first of the beatitudes. "Blessed are the poor in spirit"—the humble—"for theirs is the kingdom of heaven."

If we are to understand the shimmering of the angel, the meaning of humility, it is worth seeing how Dante uses the word in other contexts. "When I beheld Beatrice there smote into me a flame of charity so that if anyone had asked me about anything whatsoever, my reply would have been simply, *Love*, with a countenance clothed in *umiltà*." Again, "She bore about her so true an *umiltà*, that she seemed to say, *I am in peace*." Yet again, "She goes upon her way, hearing herself praised, benignly clothed with *umiltà*, and seems a thing come from heaven to earth to show forth a miracle." As Dorothy Sayers says of these examples, "The connotation is always of peace, sweetness, and a kind of suspension of the heart in a delighted tranquility." This is hardly a humility that we can think it necessary or even desirable to reject, and when we think of those around us who have been happiest it is some degree of humility in them that above all we remember. In the peace and sweetness that is described by Dante, we are far from the boasting and presumptuousness and strife of Pride. Which would a man of common sense wish to enjoy?

The foundation of humility is truth. The humble man sees himself as he is. If his depreciation of himself were untrue, as we have said, it would not be praiseworthy, and would be a form of hypocrisy, which is one of the evils of Pride. The man who is falsely humble, we know from our own experience, is one who is falsely proud. But "the saints could truthfully call themselves the greatest of sinners when they considered their great gifts from God and the inadequate return that they made." The humble man not only sees himself truthfully, he sees himself truthfully in relation to others. Without depreciating himself inappropriately, he may nevertheless be most aware of his own defects on the one hand, and on the other of the virtues of other people. He may rejoice in their gifts, while knowing how he has misused his own. In neither case will he be false.

"Dilettantism, hypothesis, speculation, a kind of amateur-search for Truth, toying and coquetting with

Truth: this is the sorest sin," said Carlyle. "The root of all other imaginable sins. It consists in the heart and soul of the man never having been open to Truth—'living in a vain show.'" One would be hard put to it to call Carlyle a humble man. But no matter. He had a way of putting his finger on aspects of the modern age that others preferred to ignore. The besetting sin of our time is that it will not take Truth with enough seriousness, as often as not with no real seriousness at all. One is not talking of credibility gaps. Neither is one talking of what may be believed by one person of another. One is speaking of a failure to acknowledge the complexity of the Truth of things and the difficulty of attaining it. In nothing is our Pride more evident than in this. We *are* nourished to toy and coquet with it. A hundred little -ologies spawn a thousand little therapies, for ourselves and our societies, and what we think we have discovered for the first time we place before all the knowledge of the past, thus further releasing ourselves to do simply what we will.

We have no humility before the past, and not much before the future either. As always when humility is absent, we stand in no truthful relation to the past, or even to the future for which we have some responsibility. We are absorbed in the present, which is only another way, but one that helps to underline the danger, of saying that we are absorbed in ourselves. We will "self-actualize" the present as we will ourselves; we will live in "now" with only the resources of now. We even refuse to listen seriously to the most truthful voice in our culture at the moment: that of a science that has learned humility in our own age and profited from it. As we find it running through the rest of the sins, it is worth considering that we may be more loveless an age than any in the past, self-sufficient in ourselves in our own time.

CHAPTER TWO
ENVY or INVIDIA

ENVY or INVIDIA

IT HAS BEEN said that Envy is the one deadly sin to which no one readily confesses. It seems to be the nastiest, the most grim, the meanest. Sneering, sly, vicious. The face of Envy is never lovely. It is never even faintly pleasant. Its expression crosses our faces in a split second. "Few are able to suppress in themselves a secret satisfaction at the misfortune of their friends," said La Rochefoucauld, and few of us are able to suppress a secret envy at someone else's good fortune, or even at someone else's good joke. If we confessed each day how often we had been envious during it, we would be on our knees longer than for any other of the sins.

Although all the deadly sins are morbid and self-destroying, Angus Wilson has said, most of the others provide at least some gratification in their early stages. But there is no gratification for Envy, nothing it can ever enjoy. Its appetite never ceases, yet its only satisfaction is endless self-torment. "It has the ugliness of a trapped rat that has gnawed its own feet in its efforts to escape." One thinks of Envy as being a drag on someone, holding him back, with no reward or pleasure or help to him. The endless self-torment is an endless self-mortification. Each of the other sins may bring what at least temporarily seem to be moments of elevation, when we think that we are set by them above other people. But the slit eyes of Envy are always turned up or aside to what it thinks is superior to it. Its posture is that of Uriah Heep. He may have been driven by others of the sins as well—Avarice, for example—but the real motive in him was Envy, which always is self-abasing. However high Envy may appear to aspire, it in fact is servile. It never straightens its back.

One of the destructive forms that Envy takes today is the widespread assumption that everyone should be able to do and experience and enjoy everything that everyone else can do and experience and enjoy. We must all plod through *The Joy of Sex* as if it is the Canadian Air Force book of exercises. "All together now! One-two-three-four!" If we hear that some people perform the sexual act while swinging from a chandelier, we feel wretched because we have not done it and we do not even have a chandelier. People who have been wholly content in their own natures, and in their expression of them, are suddenly persuaded that they have been missing something. No societies in the past have ever so assiduously taught people to envy experiences that cannot by nature be theirs. Someone once put out a parody under the title, *The Job of Sex*, and it exactly captures the arduousness of the self-torment to which Envy reduces us.

This form of Envy spreads into all our attitudes. Not only must we all be able to read poetry, which is desirable, we must all be able to write it. Time and energy are wasted in teaching "creative writing" to those who are unequipped for it; and even more time and energy are wasted in inciting children to forms of "self-expression" of which their infant natures are incapable, except on the most banal of levels, and which nourish false notions of what their adult natures might eventually become if they were realistically and intelligently directed. We are today surrounded by young people who think that they are artists and poets, because they think that they *have the right* to be artists and poets. They dabble and daub with no talent. It would be hard to count the number of them who, in the absence of a talent to write or paint, foist themselves on us as filmmakers, or who have taken up photography as an art form that will nevertheless bring a commercial reward as well. They are artists, have a right to be artists, and must be acknowledged as artists, and a camera will serve in place of any artistic vision or skill.

The legend of our times, it has been suggested, might be "The Revenge of Failure." This is what Envy has done for us. If we cannot paint well, we will destroy the canons of painting and pass ourselves off as painters. If we will not take the trouble to write poetry, we will destroy the rules of prosody and pass ourselves off as poets. If we are not inclined to the rigors of an academic discipline, we will destroy the standards of that discipline and pass ourselves off as graduates. If we cannot or will not read, we will say that "linear thought" is now irrelevant and so dispense with reading. If we cannot make music, we will simply make a noise and persuade others that it is music. If we can do nothing at all, why! we will strum a guitar all day, and call it self-expression. As long as no talent is required, no apprenticeship to a skill, everyone can do it, and we are all magically made equal. Envy has at least momentarily been appeased, and failure has had its revenge.

Envy grows naturally, said Aristotle, in relationships between equals. "We live in a society that perhaps as much as any other has pitted equals against equals," writes William F. May, but I think that he misstates his point. The United States and other Western societies are not pitting equals against equals, but unequals against unequals as if they are equals. This is a distortion of the idea of equality, and it is this distortion, as much as anything else, that has enabled the enemies of genuine equality to move to the offensive. To pit unequals against unequals as if they are equals is to make a breeding ground for Envy. The idea that we are equal has been perverted into the idea that we are identical; and when we then find that we cannot all do and experience and enjoy the things that others do and experience and enjoy, we take our revenge and deny that they were worth doing and experiencing and enjoying in the first place. What we are unable to achieve, we will bring low. What requires talent and training and hard work, we will show can be accomplished without them.

W. H. Auden once said that he could not understand the point of writing poetry if one did not obey at least the basic rules of prosody. It was like doing a crossword puzzle and, on being unable to find the correct word of seven letters, writing in one of nine letters that spills over the margin. Where is the point and satisfaction in that? The same can be asked of much of the revenge that Envy is taking today to conceal the sense of failure that gnaws at it. We are giving the name of art to what is not art, of poetry to what is not poetry, of education to what is not education, of achievement to what is not achievement, of morality to what is not morality, and of love to what is not love. We trivialize our concepts of them all, to make it seem as if we may all attain them. None of us is wholly exempt from the corruption. We find no place for the unique, for what is rare and cannot be imitated, since we would then not be able to achieve it. We seem no longer able to admire, respect, or be grateful for what is nobler or lovelier or greater than ourselves. We must pull down—or put down—what is exceptional.

What do we feel, when we feel Envy? It is not a question of seeing that someone else possesses some good, material or spiritual, and wishing that we possessed it ourselves. I may wish that I could write as well as X, or was able to afford a library like Y's, and yet not be envious of them. I feel Envy only if the facts that X writes so well, and that Y has the best editions of all the classics, make me belittle myself and my condition, and so wish to pull X and Y down. Envy is not merely a grieving on account of another's good, which is the element of Pride in it, but a grieving because one regards that good as diminishing one's own and even as reflecting disgrace on oneself. This is its essence as a sin. "Merely to grieve that one does not have something that another has is not envy," says one of the authorized handbooks of moral theology. It is a sin when the envious person wishes that the other did not have it, so that he himself "might not suffer his imaginary disadvantage." This is the canker, and we have been warned that Envy is "natural to man" (Herodotus), that it is one of the sparks that "set all on fire" (Dante), and that it is "rooted in the human heart" (Sheridan). We must be on guard against it in ourselves, but any society must be equally on guard against inciting, more than it already exists in us, a passion so universal, and one that in turn incites passions that are no less vicious. "Stirr'd with envy and revenge" is Milton's phrase, and Envy can stir up Anger and Avarice and Lust in us, and its relationship with Pride, even though a perverted form of Pride, hardly needs to be emphasized.

One of the symptoms of this Envy is dejection. It may be ceaselessly alert to what it resents, biting its nails, but as for doing something for itself, it is reduced to a kind of Sloth. (We are already seeing how closely the sins are interrelated.) The envious are filled from day to day, hour to hour, minute to minute, with a bitter regret for what they cannot have or be; and one way of at least attempting to surmount that dejection is to deny that what they lack was worth having or being in the first place. The envious person is armed with a ready malice, and if he has "a peculiar gift for chipping away at the reputations of others," if he is especially adept at noticing and pointing out their faults, that is one of his escapes from his dejection. Envy must always try to level what it cannot emulate, and one can well understand the vehemence with which the Parson in The Canterbury Tales calls it "that foul sin. . . , the worst sin there is," because it is "against all virtues and goodnesses."

One of the evils into which Envy leads us is that of backbiting. Spite, malignity, accusation. It is well understood that to take away someone's good name is second only to murder as an offense against them; it is itself a way of destroying them. The gossip column is the symbol of an envious age, and so is the contemporary form of the interview, which seems designed to ensure, in the same manner as the gossip column, that virtue and talent and achievement will be reduced to the level at which we can feel that we are their equals. They are "just like us," even a little lower than us. Nothing is allowed to seem out of the ordinary, beyond our own abilities, and even beyond our understanding. "Is nothing sacred any more?" is a cry of our age and, even allowing for the secularization of the sacred, it reaches to a particular sinfulness of Envy.

The sacred is what we cannot entirely know or master as human beings, and when we allowed a place to it in earlier ages, we did not feel the need to humble the things that we were unable to understand or control. We even realized that some things are as they are, simply as a result of fate or fortune or accident, and that they might no less deserve our respect and admiration. We can hardly expect the gossip columnists and the interviewers to put off their shoes and consider that they may be walking on holy ground. That is not what one is asking of them. But there is something sinful in an age that has spawned them and seems able only to smirk with them at whatever surpasses our own achievements.

Envy cannot bear to think that mere accident or fortune—or some other unknowable power, fate or destiny, or perhaps even God—has conferred a good on someone else. There has to be a reason, and if only it could find that reason, it persuades itself from day to day, it could also enjoy that good. This is what whets its appetite for self-torment. It will not allow for chance or admit the unknowable, so it bites its nails, believing that there is a secret that it has only to discover to succeed as another succeeds, experience as another experiences, enjoy as another enjoys. This is what is profane in Envy. It will not embrace what is fate-given, chance-given, or God-given. It will not let into its heart the notion that those of us who are only mediocre are not therefore necessarily to be counted as failures; and so it equally will not let into its heart the notion that those who excel can ungrudgingly be given our admiration and respect with no diminishing of ourselves. The envious person is moved, first and last, by his own lack of self-esteem, which is all the more tormenting because it springs from an inordinate self-love.

To criticize a public figure from deeply held political or religious, moral or aesthetic, convictions is one thing. To chip away at his or her reputation from no public belief at all is another. But our society is riddled with this kind of Envy. "The dullard's envy of brilliant men," said Max Beerbohm in *Zuleika Dobson*, "is always assuaged by the suspicion that they will come to a bad end." We feel cheated by our newspapers and magazines if no one is leveled in the dust in them. We wait in ambush for the novel that fails, for the poet who commits suicide, for the financier who is a crook, for the politician who slips, for the priest who is discovered to be an adulterer. We lie in ambush for them all, so that we may gloat at their misfortunes. It has long been recognized that *schadenfreude*—joy at the suffering of another—is peculiarly a mark of our age; but Envy makes us no less despicable—in the face of the good fortune of another, by making us capable only of despising what is admirable. There is little now that we honor.

The envious man does not love himself, although he begins with self-love. He is not grateful for, or happy in, what he is or what he has. The sin is deadly, less because it destroys him, than because it will not let him live. It will not let him live as himself, grateful for his qualities and talents, such as they are, and making the best and most rewarding use of them. His disparagement of others is a reflection of his disparagement of himself; he regards himself with as much malice as he regards them. So to torture oneself, and to torture oneself for nothing, since there is no possibility of satisfaction!—It is no wonder that Horace said that Sicilian tyrants had invented no greater torment. This is one reason why we say of Envy, perhaps more fittingly than of any other of the sins, that it is evil-minded, spiteful and given to calumny, and excited to an undue curiosity about the affairs of other people. It must justify its self-torture.

Those who try to describe Envy find that they have always to meet its eyes. The slit eyes of Envy, always they are narrowed. Envy is the evil eye, it has been said, and Dante gazes on the envious in purgatory, as if on the blind and the poor, and his imagery is terrible and excruciating, for their eyes have been closed by drawing threads of iron wire through the lids, as threads of waxed silk used to be drawn through the eyelids of a wild hawk to blind and tame it. The eyes of the envious, while they lived, could not bear to look upon joy, especially the joy of others, which might have shone on them; so now in purgatory their eyes are closed, so that they may not look on the light of the sun, and others may not look into their eyes, with the happiness that might have greeted them.

If all the sins are loveless, Envy's eyes are peculiarly so. They seem to find nothing to love in the world, not in the whole of creation, not in anyone else, not even when they are turned up to what is lovely. The other sins have been celebrated, however perversely, in popular song down the ages, but Envy has no song. It does not sing; it cannot bear to look, except through its slit eyes; it is unable to love, because it is riddled with fear. This gnawing fear that, if someone else gains something, it must be losing something, that someone else's good, material or spiritual, must mean its own lessening, runs through ourselves and our societies today. There must be a reason why it is now so unbridled. We seem to have removed the restraints on it, while at the same time increasing the provocations to it. The casualness of manners in itself removes one of the restraints. People are more ready to be bitchy about other people in public, to be heard cutting down someone else's reputation. Envy can of course still lie beneath a surface of manners, but a habit of reticence in talking about other people, which used not to be merely a surface gentility, was itself a correction of one's Envy, because one was reminded that it was not acceptable, that it was agreed that one should be ashamed of it.

Manners are not only polish; conventions are not always hypocritical; and even hypocrisy about others can serve a purpose, if it asks us to rein in our impulses, to check the "mean streak" in us, which is usually born of our Envy. Spontaneity and authenticity, those twin tempters, are not often pleasant when no bounds are set, especially over the dinner table, where the license seems now to be taken among the truffles, to bandy about the personal lives and public reputations of other people, with no obvious justification but amusement, and no apparent impulse but callousness. But restraints on our Envy can be removed in other ways. We can talk about money, or real estate, or success, subjects that used to be banned from polite tables, in such a way as to stir up Envy in us, and this at a time when our Envy of such things is provoked by our societies more than ever before.

One of the most uncomfortable facts about our economic system is that it is bound to incite Envy in those to whom it must sell. It must persuade everyone to want what everyone else has. In other words, just as Envy is a leveler, so is our commercial system a leveler: a fact that haunts its critics no less than its defenders, every socialist no less than every conservative. It has often been said that capitalism is more agitating and even revolutionary than is generally realized. It is ceaselessly provoking people to rebellion, because it is ceaselessly prodding them to Envy, to want what others have, and even to be what others are. Inevitably and restlessly, out of its own need for profit, it makes people want more than they need and have hitherto desired, and then to expect what they want. Having given them what they expect, it then incites their Envy again, to want something else.

Thoughtful conservatives are (or ought to be) among the most searching critics of our societies; and as much as anyone else today they wish to contain the malice of Envy. But every day it is stimulated by their allies in industry and commerce, as these try to sell the largest number of goods to the largest number of people, exciting a Gross National Appetite to devour the Gross National Product. This is the genius of our economic system, and there is no question that, at this level, it has conferred estimable benefits on many millions of people. But the incitement of the desire to possess goods is not in itself the incitement to Envy, but rather a provocation to Avarice and Gluttony, and it is as manifestations of these two sins that we will discuss it. As we have seen, Envy is more complex. It is a form of self-demeaning turned against others, and here the damage is done.

It has been common for conservatives in the past thirty years to complain that people in the Western democracies are increasingly filled with Envy or *ressentiment.* They have usually attributed the growth of this envious feeling to the expansion of the democratic spirit—some would say, its aggrandizement—during the past century and a half. They would certainly agree with Aristotle that Envy grows most naturally in relationships between equals, a fact that is perhaps most noticeable in the faculties of universities. There is something, of course, in all of this. Hereditary distinctions are less likely to excite Envy than any others, for example, since the elements of accident and fortune are so obvious that they can be neither a reproof nor a goad to us. There is no secret for Envy to uncover—it is out in the open; some people were high born—and we know that we cannot acquire the advantages of a long descent simply by proving our genealogy. When Melbourne said of the Order of the Garter that "there is no damned nonsense of merit about it," he was making a point we can all appreciate. Where there is no suggestion of merit, there will be little incitement to Envy. The unsuccessful man does not envy a duke. He envies the successful man, whom he thinks is otherwise "just like him," and whose success he therefore sees as a disgrace of himself.

But it is not only, perhaps not even primarily, the growth of democracy, and of the egalitarianism on which it is based, and which it in turn nourishes, that has incited to Envy. It is also in the logic of our economic system that it must do so, because this system has found no way in which to provoke people into thinking that they can have the goods that others have, without encouraging in them the accompanying belief that they are or can be as others are. Few socialist tracts are as *implicitly* and *insidiously* egalitarian as an advertisement on television; and it is an egalitarianism that, since it has no other moral or philosophical basis, must make unequals believe that they are equal in those very respects in which they are ineluctably unequal. This is one of the paradoxes of our societies: for the purposes of the economic system on which they are founded, and to that extent only, the mass market is necessarily a democratic market. Its defenders in fact talk about the "vote" of the consumer in the marketplace. Fashion used to be the preserve of wealth and privilege, but to make its profit even *haute couture* has had to cater, not to this minority, but to the department stores where "the masses" go to shop. Even it makes its goods available to all.

It is because it is philosophically opposed to equality— or says that it is—that our economic system has been unable to provide its own one-sided egalitarianism—the equality of the consumer—with any moral or philosophical foundation. Its primary achievement—and perhaps even its primary object—has therefore been to turn the discontented citizen into a contented consumer; and it then turns round in surprise when it finds that, although the consumer may indeed be satisfied, as a citizen he is still dissatisfied. It is exactly at this intersection, of the contented consumer with the discontented citizen, that Envy and *ressentiment* will breed.

We have not found it necessary to create associations and even government departments to protect the consumer because we have suddenly become more socially alert. We need them because today we are hardly citizens at all except as consumers. Everything that the thoughtful conservative now bemoans, often with justification—the weakening of social bonds, the erosion of traditional forms and values, the collapse of moral authority in society—in large part have their cause here. The citizen has not been kept abreast of the consumer. The "urban mob" to which some conservatives say that our societies have been reduced—which is a breeding ground for Envy among its atoms—has been the creation as much of our commerce as of our democracy. We may share to some extent a common activity of selling and buying in the marketplace, but beyond it we are footloose, with few traditions or values, beliefs or aspirations, pursuits or activities, that create any social bonds of much significance.

The curse of the economic system, to conservatives no less than to its critics, is that it will sell anything to anyone, and it will sell any values as well as any commodities. It is commerce that sells as art what is not art, as books what are not books, as music what is not music, as morality what is not morality, as happiness what is not happiness, even as Christmas what is not Christmas. Wherever a quick buck is to be made, it will be there like a shot, and damn the consequences to society. Once licensed by a foolishly expanded interpretation of the First Amendment, commerce is not then fastidious in the retailing of pornography. As may be seen any night on television, morally and intellectually and aesthetically, its values are determined by its need for profit. The large corporations may salve their consciences by sponsoring a few cultural programs, but these are only a gloss and have no more impact than the Surgeon General's warning on a packet of cigarettes. In the rest of their activities— the appetites they excite, the general run of the programs they sponsor, the advertising they use—they remorselessly provoke the consumer to seek an endless gratification of the very wants that they have stimulated, while the whole potential nature of the citizen is left pathetically undernourished, and even deliberately so.

These are familiar criticisms, but what we are emphasizing here is that the most destructive feeling that is excited is not acquisitiveness, but a sourness of feeling in people whose own personalities, simply as human beings, are given no real satisfaction or acknowledgment, irrespective of such talents or capacities or ambitions as they may possess. Fundamentally what we mean by equality is that everyone should be given an equality of consideration. But this is precisely what our societies do not do in their neglect of the individual as a citizen. While the Christian message was believed, it at least carried the reassurance that one was equal in the eyes of someone, that somewhere one was of as much consequence as others in the final order of things, even if that somewhere was in another world. Even the lowliest could help to build Chartres Cathedral, or enter it, and feel that he was an intelligible part of a universe that was itself intelligible, of which his society was a part, and there is perhaps no more important way in which consideration can be shown to a human being.

The belief might be built on what we would today

regard as meager data. But we are in no position to despise it. We no longer believe that somewhere we may enjoy an equality of consideration as citizens in the City of God. All we have is right here. And right here our societies show little interest in nourishing us as citizens, of giving an equal consideration to our whole natures as men and women who form an intelligible part of an order that is also intelligible. We cannot ask people to live so pointlessly, and yet to live with purpose, to strive to do good and not to do evil, and to respect their societies when these show them scant respect. No society can ask respect when it gives it members no self-respect. Human beings in this condition cannot know themselves as human beings, and they will turn haplessly into selfish and resentful helots, Envy goading them.

There is another incitement to Envy in our societies. Not only they, but all of what we rather charitably call our political philosophies, are based on the idea of meritocracy: the notion that merit should be discovered, selected, and trained, in our schools and our universities, and then elevated to positions of power and influence, again by a process of competition, with the rewards and honors that are considered to be appropriate. What system would be more fair or more intelligible, how could there be a more rational or just way of doing things? But there is a worm at its core. A system of elites that are, or are supposed to be, chosen on merit must rest on two assumptions: that everyone begins with an equal chance from the same starting line, and that the rules of the competition are fair at every stage. These conditions are in fact unrealizable, which is the flaw in the idea that "equality of opportunity" is adequate as a prescription. Unrealizable or not, what matters here is that the idea of merit is rooted in the idea of equality. Its ultimate moral sanctions are that people start equal and that they have an equal chance at every stage in the race. It therefore has to meet the leveling spirit of Envy, when someone asks why he did not make it to the top, instead of someone else who is "just like him," for Envy will not accept the explanation that the successful person was more talented than he, and in fact deserved to succeed.

This is the curse of a system that is based on merit. It produces an inequality of results, as it is intended to do, but it can justify itself only by appealing to the idea of equality, to the very impulse that it would like to allay. There could be no more certain prescription for inciting people to Envy, for it leaves the majority of them, who do not succeed, with no alternative but to see themselves as losers. In an equal race, as they have been told it is, they were defeated. If it is merit alone that is rewarded, as they have again been told, then they have been proved to have little or none. But one cannot ask people to accept so sweeping and blindfold a dismissal of their own abilities, and this is one reason why what is so pretentiously described as a meritocracy is popularly described as a rat race. Those who are content with a system of "equality of opportunity" on the terms that now exist, and defend it as rational and fair, must face the fact that it is as a rat race that it is perceived, and that as such it cannot be expected to inspire either virtue or allegiance, in those who either win or lose.

The rat race is the vivid popular description of a system of promotion and rewards that appeals to Avarice, of course, but to an even stronger motive in Envy. It is not really for the additional material rewards that a man near the top will set his mouth and slit his eyes in order to get even nearer to it still. It is Envy that spurs him. He cannot live contentedly, his talents fittingly employed in some satisfying task, if a colleague rises to a vice-presidency. He will even struggle to exchange a worthwhile job as the head of a department for nothing more than the prestige that attaches to a vice-president of his corporation, and his most powerful motive is that he does not wish to appear or to feel disgraced by the advancement of someone else. At a level of society where leaders should be bred who understand and relish its values, we find instead only people whose cynicism is sharper and more grating than it is in those below them. If our societies lack the authority that should be earned by respect, it is partly because those at the top do not themselves respect it.

This spirit of Envy is bred early into those who are groomed to succeed and lead. A young man from Harvard Law School, say, has a peculiarly ferocious ambition. He has left the pasture where the grass could hardly be greener for a young colt, and he enters the world to advance and to conquer with his talents and his training. One would expect him to be filled with a gladitorial zeal as he begins his career, to feel that he can dare to challenge the society that he aspires to lead, to have a warmth of conviction that he can bring to it the messages of truth and beauty, sweetness and light, for which it has been waiting for so long. But, no! He talks only about the status and earnings of his elders on whose heels he is treading, and of his peers who seem at the first throw of the dice to have landed the most prestigious and best-paying jobs. He is already sour at the prospect of the race that he has begun, even while the dew of his youthfulness is still moist on his cheeks. Watch him and listen to him carefully. Envy is already in him, the turn of his mouth, his turns of phrase. An education that is intended to breed the leaders of a society with strongly held and individual values, has pupped instead a litter of young people who are already disillusioned with it at the first encounter.

There is little wrong with the competitive spirit, if it is kept within bounds, but everything wrong with the envious spirit; and it is the second that our societies and especially our schools, far more than in the past, seem bent on nourishing in order later to exploit. The collapse of the professions has been largely the result of the insinuation of the spirit of Envy into them. The professions were the true leaders of a middle-class society, when that society still had confidence in its own values. The doctors and the teachers and the ministers were the leaders of opinion in villages, in small towns, in neighborhoods in the large cities, not very well paid and not even with much wordly prestige, but enjoying a deserved respect in their communities, which in turn earned them a deserved authority. Now they are well paid, in comparison with the past, and they enjoy no respect and have ceased to be leaders. They no longer stand inside their societies, but at the same time as the exemplars of the values that society is most likely to let slide; they have become mere mercenaries of their societies, like others, the exemplars of everything in them that corrupts and, if not challenged, is bound to corrupt even the best that they can produce.

This is the work of Envy, let loose in our societies as never in the past. The university teacher used to be modestly and even ill paid, but he was ambitious to teach well and, teaching well, he stood high in the respect of others and in his own self-respect. He even had the respect of his pupils. Now he is well paid; in most cases, grossly overpaid; he does not teach well; and he enjoys little respect from others, and if honest with himself has even less self-respect. He has little authority in the classroom, in the university as a whole, or in the wider community, and he is gnawed by the sneaking suspicion that he is a charlatan. He quickly grows bilious in temper. He takes up any cause that sets out to diminish such authority as there may still be elsewhere, which is a constant provocation to his own wretched lack of authority. Enjoying little respect from his pupils, he seeks instead their approval, while knowing that their approval is an ultimate expression of their disdain. If you can't beat them, join them: Such is the callowness of his posture. Driven by Envy to these extremities, Envy continues to breed ever more malignantly and destructively in him.

They are a vociferous part of what Irving Kristol calls the "new class," the *literati* of various levels of untutored and undirected intelligence, and as usual he has a point to be answered, which is as much as one is entitled to ask of anyone. But he talks of this "new class" as if their pettiness and malignancy came only from themselves, no more than a sickness of the individual, as if our societies have played no part in nourishing in them their mean-spiritedness and lack of any real seriousness of purpose. One might say of them that they are empty, as the professions have never been before, of the Roman virtues of *pietas, dignitas,* and *gravitas,* but one must at once ask where these virtues are to be found, most of all to be found celebrated and instilled, in the societies that have nourished this "new class." These are envious people—teachers, writers, journalists, publicists, broadcasters, dependents on foundations, dependents on grants, art students, artists, ministers, physicists, actors, directors, filmmakers—but they have been bred by Envy. For them as for others, our societies have supplied no motive for simply doing what they do well, but only the prod of Envy.

One of the evils of Envy, says the theologian, is that it is a source of discord. We hardly need him to tell us; we know it in ourselves and in our everyday lives. Envy is a sower of strife, between colleagues, between neighbors, even between friends, and here it is close to Pride. It introduces into even the most straightforward of relationships an atmosphere of distrust, of ill-ease and contention and malice, until even the most amiable and complaisant of people will find in self-defense that they also have fangs. It is also—and here one may admire the precision of the vocabulary to which theology so often reaches—the source of *murmuring*. No sooner is it said than one hears the sound of murmuring in one's own day, as Envy does its work, and laps-laps-laps against the few shore-defenses we have built around us, eroding them slowly but certainly, whispering its doubts and suspicions and gossip, until we begin to believe and look forward to them.

We learn to envy not only those who have got to the top, whatever the reasons for their success, and not only those who are more able than us, but even those who are more virtuous. We even envy someone who is good! We will not believe that they are good, or that they are as good as they seem, or that they are good for the right reasons. If they are not simply hypocritical, there must be an ulterior motive, or some psychological complex. The good man must be bad inside. The good marriage must be subject to strains that are hidden from us. The good worker must be psychologically submissive. The good shepherd must have transferred his capacity to love human beings to his sheep. Goodness is painted as bad.

The Envy of another's spiritual gifts has always been regarded in theology as a grievous sin. As St. John of the Cross put it: "As far as envy is concerned, many experience displeasure when they see others in the possession of spiritual goods. They feel sensibly hurt because others surpass them on this road, and they resent it when others are praised." This, however, is quite contrary to love which, as St. Peter says, rejoices in goodness. "And if love has envy, it is a holy envy; for love grieves at not possessing the virtues of others, but it rejoices that another person possesses them." Few of us are capable of such a rejoicing all the time. We know how Envy works in us, how it works in our age, how it works in our own gossip as well as in the gossip columns that we read precisely with an invidious spirit. But even as we feel acutely the personal devastation that it wreaks, we cannot exonerate our societies from all responsibility.

The correction of Envy in theology lies in our love of God, whose meaning even the irreligious can understand and to some extent emulate, our love of our neighbor as ourselves, and of course our love of our enemies. The Devil is "wounded to the death by love for our enemies," says the Parson in his tale; and where the envious repent in purgatory, Dante finds that the cords that bring them to their penitence are drawn by "charity's correcting hand." But what do our societies bid us love? To what do they encourage us to be charitable? These are barely even concepts any longer in our societies, and in our private lives they are hardly more than arrangements of convenience, transactions with others in our immediate environment, that offer some emotional servicing when we need it. Our word for love now is therapy. Our word for charitableness now is massage.

We are not taught to love the past. We take from it what we think is useful to us, and discard and disdain the rest. We are not taught to love the ancients. We feel reproached by the sternness of their biddings, and flee the challenge of their certainties. We are not taught to love the saints. They are too awkward for us in their intensity, and we find a psychological explanation for their readiness to serve. We are not taught to love the prophets. They do not allow us to whiffle away our present, but snatch from us our golden calves and summon us to some strenuous endeavor for a future we will not see. We are not taught to love our heroes. They were straw men, with papier-mâché masks. We are not taught to love our institutions. They threaten our spontaneity and authenticity, those twin betrayers as well as tempters, on which we giddily lean, and ask from us obligations in return for the rights they bestow and protect. What other than ourselves do we love? In all of these we can feel Pride working through the malice of Envy.

Even our socialism has become more loveless than in

the past and makes its appeal primarily to our Envy. There is a fatal socialism that merely wishes to pull a few people down, rather than pull a large number up; and although throughout its history it has seldom come fully to grips with the Envy that the leveling impulse will always too easily incite, socialism has seldom before been so generally mean-spirited and at the same time self-righteous in its claims. In our Western societies today it is too exclusively interested in the redistribution of material goods. It is as if it has been corrupted by its enemy, by the success of our present societies in creating populations of consumers who are more or less gratified in their consuming, and so reduced itself to saying merely that it will supply the same gratifications more justly to more people. This is a program with no vision. Whether or not it is socialism, it is certainly neither the criticism nor the reformation that our societies so desperately need, if we are to be uplifted by them.

If there is no check to our Envy in our societies, it is because there is nothing that they teach us, or can even show us, to honor more than we honor ourselves. Deprived of saints and prophets and heroes, even of public figures of standing, we find a substitute for them in the celebrity. The celebrity is the creature of an envious age. He is someone to whom we ascribe no virtuousness, whose talents are not of primary interest, whom we do not think of as wise beyond us, or generous beyond us, or selfless beyond us, or dedicated beyond us, or even hardworking beyond us. He is merely paid beyond us. In our Envy we erect them, for a while let our Envy prey on them, and then in our Envy destroy them. Envy could ask for no more slavish creature. The talk shows on television are feasts for our Envy. The audience is the tyrant, fickle as tyrants by nature are, and the celebrities are fed to it, for it to devour and then call monstrously for another.

What more could Envy ask to appease its torment?

What it sets up as greater than it, it shows to be even less than its equal. It does not wish to be shown what is nobler or more virtuous than it, and our societies cannot be left blameless for creating populations of helots, who then debase everything to the level of vulgarity to which they have been cynically tutored. We cannot excuse the supposed leaders of those societies, who pay extravagant sums for novels that are no more than trash, not to sell them as trash, which is at least an old form of harlotry, but to sell them and review them and acclaim them as works of literature. For our writers are then hardly resistant to Envy and persuade themselves that if such works can, not only command a huge advance on royalties, but actually be honored by reviews that take them seriously, they may as well emulate what seems to bring no disgrace with its fee. It is not only the individuals who are at fault; their societies are egging them on with a reckless disregard for any real standards.

Envy has been allowed to become one of the governing motives of our societies, more than of any in the past, perverting the idea of equality, debasing the institutions and modest ambitions of democracy, debilitating the notion of excellence and even achievement, corrupting any elevated sense of our public life, and leaving the citizens to a simultaneously excited and dejected pursuit of what has been contemptously brought down to the level of their assumed capacities. It is no wonder that Angus Wilson has said that Envy wears "an uglier face than Lust's bloodshot eyes, or Gluttony's paunch, or Pride's camel nose, or Avarice's thin lips." It is a more secret appetite than these and reigns more secretly in us. But it also reigns more secretly in our societies, which have discovered that it may ceaselessly be incited and with profit appeased, to be incited again and then appeased once more with the profit undiminished, to replace any more strenuous longings or aspirations that might inspire us.

While the spirit of Envy is loose in our societies, it can

reduce our ambitions only to meanness and pettiness, to the desire, not so much to do well ourselves, as to see others do worse. This malice and evilmindedness are in ourselves, a habitual sin, but never have our societies so conspired to inflame them in us. If all the sins are a hardening of the heart, Envy is also a bitterness of the heart; and if we are alienated and sullen and feckless, it is partly because, with enough of our humanity still flickering in us, we can only regard with renewed bitterness the waste of the bitterness of heart to which we have already been reduced.

CHAPTER THREE
ANGER or IRA

ANGER or IRA

HOW ODD WE can feel—even preposterous—when we have been angry. What was it all about? Where did it come from? "I forgive myself" a friend of mine will say the next day, and it seems enough; at least he is not asking one to forgive him. Such outbursts are not to be taken lightly. We fling words in anger and, when words are flung, they have a way of finding a perhaps unintended but wide-open target. After all, if we are spraying the whole landscape with gunshot, the odds are that we will score a hit somewhere. Anger is adept with menace and accusation. Our voices rise. Our eyes blaze. Our bodies stiffen. Our fingers point. Our feet stamp. Our words are hurled. "You . . . You . . . YOU," rising in pitch, spatters our diatribe. We are trying to make an enemy, even when there is none, and the sad thing is that we may succeed. Whoever said that sticks and stones may break our bones, but words can never hurt us, must have lived among deaf mutes. Careless words can do untold damage; one word may destroy even a sublime love. Anger may not always cause a deep wound, but it must leave a residue of hatred in the end, and a desire for revenge. The enemy whom it at first invented will have been stung into existence by its tongue.

Our flashes of anger are not blameless, but it is assumed that our reason has not assented to them. They are regarded therefore as a venial sin. What is more, there may be something to be said for them, for from time to time, "getting it off one's chest." Some years ago a group of British and American psychologists and social workers met at the Tavistock Institute in London to compare notes on the condition of the contemporary family. One American psychologist said that the main sound she associated with the British family was that of doors being banged inside it, whereas the main sound she associated with the American family was that of cars being driven away from outside it. The American family seems sometimes to try too hard to bypass anger, and this may well be a reason why in the wider society, where adults deal with adults, there are occasionally such inexplicable and destructive outbursts of anger. The child needs to learn, not only how to control its anger, but how sometimes to express it. Anger needs a safety valve, before it accumulates and at last breaks out, to cause the devastation of which it is capable.

Nevertheless, as we describe the Anger that is counted as a deadly sin, we will find that we return constantly to our everyday outbursts of anger for our illustrations. They are the reminder, with their strutting and posturing, of how deeply the sin is embedded in us. The tantrum of the child is natural to it, before any other of the sins, with the exception only of Pride. When its will meets the boundaries that are set to it, it dissolves into tears, which can be filled sometimes with the most subtle menaces of Anger. It howls and screams. We often say that an outburst of anger in the adult is mere childishness, and we should not refuse our own insights. We are saying that the child also and already sins.

But it is not our flashes of anger, at least in themselves, that are counted as one of the deadly sins. Anger as a deadly sin is "a disorderly outburst of emotion connected with the inordinate desire for revenge"; and it may be inordinate "either in regard to the object on which [it] is vented, or in the degree in which [it] is fostered or expressed." It is likely to be accompanied by surliness of heart, by malice aforethought, and above all by the determination to take vengeance; and since it is sustained over a length of time, we are likely to have assented to it with our reason, and then with our will, which are two of the conditions of all sinning: that we do it knowingly and willingly.

William F. May gives the name of Hatred to the sin of Anger, to emphasize that it takes hold of us "in the highest reaches of the mind," that it becomes an obsession, that once it has taken hold it endures. The point is important, but Hatred is the wrong word. Hatred is not the same as Anger, although it is a large component of it. It is often one (but only one) of its motives, and is unavoidably one of its consequences. If we are to give Anger another name, to emphasize its character, we should stick to the family of its close relatives. We may call it Wrath, which carries the same suggestion of an obsession, of something that consumes us, not the flash of lightning, the sudden clap of thunder, but a burning in us like a banked fire. Wrath is a fixation. Its eyes are set on the object of its anger. It devours itself and others. It lays waste. A modern symbol of it is the policy of the scorched earth in war.

We think of Anger in terms of fire: blazing, flaming, scorching, smoking, fuming, spitting, smoldering, heated, white hot, simmering, boiling, and even when it is ice-cold it will still burn. It has been called the Devil's furnace, and the other sins will fuel it. Pride can obviously lead to Wrath; scorn and obstinacy, for example, are associated with them both. So also can Envy, with its own eyes fixed on the object of its resentment, seeking vengeance. Avarice may easily lead to it, if it is balked; and if it also is balked, Lust can lead to it. But in its turn Wrath will inflame the other sins. The angry man is likely to become more proud, more envious, more avaricious, and he may even become more slothful, attending less than he should to other things, since his Wrath consumes him. Flames lick and leap anywhere they find something to burn. A fire may smolder for a long time unnoticed. So can Wrath burn its way through a whole being, into his words and deeds and gestures; and no other of the sins uses all three of these so skillfully, or in so deadly a combination.

We understand that there are angry people, who seem simply to be angry, within themselves, at anything and everything: angry at life, angry at their lot, angry at the world, angry at everyone else, and angry at themselves, although this they do not see. It is hardly worth asking them the cause, because they will always be angry at something. Show them that there is no reason for Anger in one circumstance, they will return the next day with their Anger still justified, and sometimes they seem most mild. These are people of Wrath, sustained and vengeful. We should be warned by them because, even if it may only be occasionally, the same Anger can work also in us and cause its own harm.

We live in an age of Wrath. It is to be found in the terrorist, the kidnapper, the hijacker, the looter, and in the clenched fist of the demonstrator. One mentions these at the beginning only because they are the most obvious symbolic figures. They are not alone. When we ask what is their justification, they hardly have to give an answer, because our age finds it for them. *They are angry.* That is apparently enough. We justify their Wrath, so we justify their violence. If someone thinks that he has cause to be angry, he may act from his Anger as destructively as he sees fit. In fact, we have come close to the point of giving to Wrath an incontestable license to terrorize our societies, just as an angry man may terrorize his family, but whereas we do not excuse the husband or the father, we extend our sympathy and understanding to the terrorist.

The police stand by while mayhem is committed in the most literal sense. Mayhem is "the malicious and permanent deprival of another of the use of a member of his body resulting in impairing his fighting ability and constituting a grave offense under English common law." This is exactly what happens when a society has been terrorized into surrendering its right to protect itself, by restraining its police from lawful actions, out of the fear that they might provoke those who are terrorizing it to even more violence and destruction. The society has allowed its fighting ability to be impaired, maliciously and permanently, on the ground that, just as Wrath must be given our understanding, so the violence to which it leads must be given our tolerance. But it is more than understanding and tolerance that we give so generously. It is we in our societies who have supplied the excuse— not only the excuse, but even the stimulus—who have not only encouraged the Wrath, but provoked people to it.

Societies that tolerate and encourage so destructive a force within their own bodies must at some point have taken a wrong turning, and we have given Wrath its license by elevating a concept of individual and human rights that is flagrantly misleading. Any felt need or desire or longing, for anything that one lacks but someone else has, is today conceived to be a right that, when demanded, must be conceded without challenge. And if it is not at once conceded, the claimants are entitled to be angry, just as a child might be thought to be entitled to be angry if it is not allowed to play with a bone china plate that belongs to its parents. We can hardly blame the claimants for taking advantage of this foolishness, since they are justified in advance on four grounds: what they want, it is their right to have; when it is asked, it should be granted; if it is not granted, it is understandable that they are angry; since they are angry, it is clear that their demand in the first place was justified. (Lest it be thought that no one could seriously support such logic, let it be said that this has for the past decade been very much the gospel of Tom Wicker and of others contributing to the *New York Times*.) No civilized societies can ever before have trapped themselves into such a vicious circle, so that any and every felt want is translated into an alleged right, inciting its citizens to Anger and then to its destructiveness.

Carried to its most extreme and ludicrous in recent years, there have been women who have seemed to be claiming, not merely the rights that men enjoy as citizens, but the right themselves to be men; students who have actually been claiming the right to be their own educators, not only choosing what they will study, which is a curious license in the first place, but even choosing their own teachers and grading them; and children who have been claiming the right to be adults, until our newspapers began to report solemnly that there were "student rights" movements at the grade school level. All of these absurdities have resulted in various expressions of Wrath, which have in turn provoked various degrees of violence. They may seem only to be follies, but follies can harm. One draws attention to them only to emphasize that there are no boundaries that can logically be set to the concept of individual and human rights that we have so frivolously adopted. Any of us may simply express a felt need or want as a right, and our societies have left themselves with little or no rebuttal.

If we are to confront this question of rights, we need to take the most complex and searching of issues. The right to have "control over one's own body," for example, which is used to justify "abortion on demand," as if abortion is a service that one should be able to get from Sears & Roebuck or through a mail order catalog, is a right that not even men enjoy. If we drive on the wrong side of the road, our bodies are forcibly removed from it; if we punch an innocent stranger on the nose, our bodies are forcibly restrained. We are not allowed to walk naked in the streets, or to perform the sexual act on the counter of a public bar or in the aisle of a crowded aircraft, and of course the male body is not allowed to rape when it feels the hapless urge. There are people who would like to prevent us from smoking, because it is bad for our bodies, and there are laws against the use of some drugs for the same reason. Even biologically we do not have control of our own bodies. They are subject to infection, virus, disease, decay, and death. There will be angry complaints—they will of course be angry—that these are a *reductio ad absurdum*. But it is necessary to make the point, because one cannot claim as a right what cannot be guaranteed, and there is no way of guaranteeing to any of us, male or female, the right to have "control over our own bodies." To present as rights what cannot in the end be secured as rights, as we all too often do today, is as sure a prescription for Wrath as any other that could be proposed.

If our bodies are subject to disease, decay, and death, they are no less subject to impulse, whim, and passion, to those very moments when we in fact say that we have lost control of ourselves. (The control has not been taken away from us, we have surrendered it.) Most unwanted pregnancies are themselves a result of a woman having lost control of her own body—to impulse, whim, passion, or lust—and the demand for nontherapeutic abortions is a demand only to remove the consequences of having previously forfeited control over her own body, which she now imagines she may reassert with surgical assistance from someone else. The Wrath with which the demand for nontherapeutic abortions is sometimes made—a Wrath that is inevitably directed, even if not intentionally, at an innocent object, the conceived child—is the result of conferring on merely felt wants the character of rights. If one wants (or feels that one needs) to get rid of a fetus, then one apparently has the indefeasible right to get rid of it. There may or may not be a case for allowing women to have nontherapeutic abortions on demand. That is not the question that is being argued here. One is merely saying that to translate a woman's wish to have an abortion into her right to have it is merely another example—and an extreme one—of the absurdly distorted concept of individual and human rights by which our societies are now confused, and we are in this way set against each other in an endless combat for the rights we claim. Anger comes.

Most of the rights that someone claims will, if granted, involve the diminishing of another's rights. The freedom of a woman to choose not to have a child can be a diminishing of the freedom of a man to enjoy the child whom he played some part in conceiving. Let us suppose that a young man and a young woman decide that they will have a child, that they then conceive one, but that the woman is then offered a good job that she has always wanted. She decides to abort the fetus, even though the man still wishes to have the child, and can point out that it is as much "his" as it is "hers," that it was conceived equally by them by a joint decision and a joint act, presumably of love for each other and for the child that may be a creation of it. (One is deliberately taking an example in which the "rights" are in some real balance, because it is in such cases that one can see the issues that are involved.) We have not even raised the question of the rights that the fetus may have—the crux of the matter— because we are pointing out only that so slipshod a concept of individual rights as we have adopted, with scarcely any resistance, can lead only to situations in which a discord that is so deep that it can hardly be spoken is incited on both sides.

Even if we put aside for a moment the violence of feeling to which such a concept can lead, we can see in other forms the discord that it incites. We may even see it more clearly in them, precisely because the question of Wrath does not so obviously intrude. American courts have in the past ten years been inundated by cases of alleged discrimination: not discrimination on the grounds of someone's race or religion or sex, but discrimination on almost any ground that the plaintiffs and their lawyers have the ingenuity to concoct. Two high school students were refused permission to publish an article on birth control in their high school newspaper. They took the case to the courts on the grounds that they were being discriminated against because they were not adults, and the Fourth Circuit Court of Appeals agreed with them. A high school student "as a joke" pushed a chocolate cream pie into the face of one of her teachers and in punishment was not allowed to attend her graduation. She took her case to the courts on the grounds that she was being discriminated against, because the punishment had been decided without a hearing before the county school authorities. At least in this case, the suit was rejected. Other students have complained that they have been discriminated against for wearing blue jeans or not wearing shoes.

There have been thousands of cases brought by adults on grounds that are hardly less frivolous, until some lawyers now reasonably ask: If everyone can claim that they are being discriminated against on almost any ground, then what is *not* discrimination and (even more puzzling) what *is* discrimination? If everyone can claim that they are the victims of discrimination, then clearly there is no longer any discrimination. This is only another way of saying what we have been suggesting here. If everyone can claim that any felt want or need or longing is a right, there are clearly no such things as rights left at all, since everyone's supposed rights are pitted legitimately against everyone else's supposed rights, and we no longer have any way of deciding what is a right and what is not. These cases may seem now to be harmlessly in the courts, but the assumptions behind them can only breed discord, which in turn can only breed a violent society. We have it now.

No sooner did the young begin claiming their rights against the adults ahead of them, than the old came forward to claim their rights against the adults behind them. In the past five years the number of complaints which the Department of Labor has received of discrimination on the grounds of age has multiplied six times. When the young and the old have established their claims, the adults in the middle will arrive with their own, just as the whites have brought their claims of reverse discrimination against the blacks. There is no way in which a society that rests on such premises can in the end breed anything but the discord of Anger. When an FBI agent sues the FBI on the grounds that his rights were violated, because he was censured and transferred to a different post for living with a woman out of wedlock, he is acting as someone who has been taught by his society that he has, in any and every situation as he chooses to define it, the right to act and live exactly as he pleases, even if it is against the rules or standards of the organization to which he belongs of his own free will. If this right is denied, he believes he has the right to be angry. He has not even learned the wisdom of Groucho Marx, that a club that will have one as a member is not worth joining.

If people have been taught to believe that they have the right to something that they happen to desire, and this alleged right is not granted, it is inevitable that they will at some point yield to anger; and in then seeking to take the alleged right for themselves, they will easily be tempted to seek revenge. The desire for revenge is both one of the impetuses to Wrath, and one of its consequences. This is true even in our outbursts at people we know; for one reason or another we are trying to "get back" at them. When we are consumed with Wrath, not only are our eyes fixed with hatred on the enemy, but we become preoccupied with stratagems of revenge. When we watch someone who is angry, we often say that he is out of his mind. He is driven out of it by the thirst for revenge, and the lengths and strategies to which it impels him. We know it even in our own outbursts. The position in which we put ourselves is impossible, and we seek revenge on others even for that.

Whether with deeds or words, the wish is to harm another. But our fixation also harms us when we succumb to it. It makes us imagine slights and injuries where there are none, and to feel an undue indignation at them. When we say that someone is quick to anger, we do not mean only that he gets angry quickly, but that he gets angry at things that do not deserve such vehemence. We usually feel a little shamefaced after we have been angry with someone. Why did so small an incident—a pair of socks that were mislaid—trigger so violent a reaction? Why did we throw everything but the kitchen sink into our tirade? But this is even more true of the sustained Wrath that has its eyes fixed relentlessly on its enemy. To the real injuries that have been done to us, we add slights and injuries that are imaginary, and these tend to dominate our minds. It is always easy to itemize the small and imagined hurts, and scream "You . . . You . . . YOU" in accusation as we number them off. But the causes and nature of the larger and more genuine hurts are more complex, and it is not in Anger that we can counter them most effectively. Many of the liberation movements and especially their extreme wings, acting from Wrath and a desire for revenge, fixing their eyes on the imaginary rather than the real injuries, the small rather than the large, have hurt themselves even more than others by the disproportion of their acts.

But we are harmed in an even deeper way. In our obsession with the enemy, we tend to become the enemy. The story of the Resistance was a story of courage, yes, but it was a story also of a Wrath that became self-justifying, prepared to use and even refine some of the enemy's methods. Nazism in the end had its victories, not as a direct result of its own barbarism, for this was defeated, but in the barbarism that it inspired in its opponents, because they were victorious. It was then a small jump from the Resistance to the terrorist—all guerilla movements are a form of arbitrary violence that has been given a license—and from the terrorist to his fellows—the kidnapper and the hijacker—whose violence is peculiarly vile because it is especially cowardly. It is since World War II that the idea of a self-legitimizing terrorism has been given an idly tolerant acquiescence by our civilization. Either the injuries of the centuries or the injury of the moment, real or imagined, are thought to be enough of a warrant for any violence; and we are always surprised at the end of the day, when we have permitted or resorted to such methods, to find that they have not left us untouched. If we have used them, even our victory will not be intact. We may have terrorized at the moment, like the head of a family, but it is we who lose in the end.

The slave will not be free until he has ceased to direct his mind and his actions against the slaveowner, until he rids himself of the slaveowner as the enemy who defines him. The strength of this old truth has been no less obvious in the liberation movements in the past two decades. There came a vital point in the development of the black movement, at the end of the 1960s and the beginning of the 1970s, when the blacks in America put "honky" out of their minds. It became possible to say that black is beautiful, without having to snarl that white is ugly. This was indeed a moment of self-liberation. But the women's movement has not yet wholly freed itself from a preoccupation with the male as a real or supposed oppressor and so still puts itself too often into the position of seeking a futile vengeance at the cost of the genuine progress that has yet to be made. The homosexual who said to the *New York Times* in 1977, "I can get my windows washed by a gay person, my television repaired, do anything, and never see a straight person again," had his eyes fixed remorselessly on the heterosexual as his enemy, in hatred and with a desire for vengeance; and in so misdirecting his energies he diminishes himself as a human being, even while he says that it is as a human being that he wishes to be recognized. He still has the mentality and spirit of a slave.

It will be said that all liberation or revolutionary movements have to go through an extreme and violent phase. Even if this were true, such phases are still wasting and distorting, likely to corrupt, and the necessity for them is the result of the sinfulness of our natures. We turn to vengeance and violence, because we are unable to check our Wrath and are unwilling and unable to find a better way. This way has been shown to us, and we know in our right reason it is better. The injunction to love our enemies as ourselves is again the correction that we need. But we find it difficult to follow, hard even to make the attempt. To love our enemies as ourselves is to look upon them with charity and to see that they are driven by the same frailty and inclination to evil that beset us all. Yet we do not easily do this, even though it can be shown from a thousand examples, in history and in our own lives, that those who do not love their enemies as themselves, who do not fight them with forgiveness already in their hearts, are incapable also of loving their neighbors as themselves. The extremist leaders of revolutionary movements seldom love their followers. They may call them their comrades; there is little of the affection of comradeship in them. When the revolution has been won and they sit in the seats of power, they regard their followers with the same bitterness of heart as earlier they regarded their enemies.

"Blessed are the peacemakers, for they shall be called the children of God." Blessed are the peacemakers, the Parson adds in his tale, for they know not evil wrath. Indeed the prescriptions of the Sermon on the Mount must seem beyond our reach. But we need to emphasize what was said in the first of these essays: that to make the effort, to know but not to be dismayed by our own inadequacy and backsliding, is the beginning of righteousness, of the correction that we need, and this we can manage. The effort at goodness, no less than the surrender to evil, can become a habit, and little by little it will help to restore us. When once the effort has been made to love an enemy, it is easier the next time, and it is we who feel restored, perhaps even more than the enemy. A child who has stamped to its room in anger and closed the door, or been sent to it until it is contrite, finds it difficult to open the door and come out; it sits there and banks the fires of its misery, even as it still stokes the fires of its vengefulness, and does not know how to return civilly to the company it has left. It is one of the evidences of our adulthood that we know how to come out of that room, how to apologize and forgive with civility and graciousness and even humor—in short, how to love our enemy, even of the moment—and the restoration that is then felt, by all who are concerned, tells of more than a correction. For what has been demonstrated is the power, whenever it is exercised, that we know that love possesses.

For two centuries we have lived in an age of revolutions, and whatever the good they may have brought, they have singly and cumulatively rendered our perceptions of our societies and of ourselves more impoverished, and made us less eager and able to choose to act rightly. Too many sophistries have for too long told us that violence is not violence, cruelty is not cruelty, torture is not torture, evil is not evil, if these are committed in the name of some virtue that is discovered and extolled by the revolution. When the political and social considerations have been set aside and we face the moral choices that are set before us, we barely know how to distinguish between good and evil if a revolutionary banner is held above us. But the issues ultimately are moral. And in an age in which so many people angrily claim the rights that they think are properly theirs, with little thought of the obligations that are attached to them and alone give them any moral substance, we need to recover the sense that the pressing of such claims does not necessarily need, and is usually harmed by, a resort to extremism and violence, which are themselves only euphemisms for cruelty of various forms and degrees. We have got into the habit of thinking that only the extremist "keeps the faith," but the history of every revolutionary or liberation movement of the past two centuries is there to show the opposite: that it is the extremists who are usually the betrayers of the faith, and of all the motives in them that works the corruption, none is stronger than the Wrath that they will not check.

Something more lies behind the Anger that has been loosed in our age. One of the most common provocations to anger in our day-to-day relationships is a sudden onrush of fear, and one of the most common causes of this fear is that we are anxious not to be shown to be ignorant. We are all in some way afraid of what we do not know, and we do not like our ignorance being brought to our own or to anyone else's attention. If someone says that we are misusing a word and points to the definition in the dictionary, we angrily retort that we have the right to use words as we choose; if someone tries to rebut us with a passage from Aristotle, we say with heat that he lived more than two thousand years ago, and so cannot speak to us with any meaning today; if we know nothing of modern science, we vehemently meet an appeal to it by denying its relevance. If this is true in our lives from day to day, it is no less true beyond them. We feel threatened in our societies now by the evidence of superior knowledge—so much knowledge that most of it is unavailable to even the most intelligent of us—and our fear of it moves us to a deep Wrath that we do not completely recognize.

Montaigne quotes a classical author who said that the wisest of men is the peasant, because he knows what he needs to be wise about. As long as he knows the seasons, his soil, his crops, his animals, the weather, he needs to be wise about nothing else, except his God, and his God is all about him, in the earth and the sky, and in the cycle of each year. The peasant is not bothered by the classier knowledge of the cities, and he is traditionally slow to anger. But in our cities, we seem no longer to know what we need to know. Do we need to know everything about black holes, about cancer, about the neutron bomb, about Zaire, about laetrile, about suntan lotions, about Norman Mailer, about art, about astrophysics, about biochemistry, about the world, about the universe, about life, about death, about God? What in all this can we hope to be wise about?

To do even the simplest thing, we hardly seem to know what we need to know. A child will strain its eyes at the small print on the wrapping before it buys a candy bar and, instead of sitting at the soda fountain with its friends, will exchange scientific reports with the pharmacist about which toothpaste is most likely to reduce cavities. Not only do we feel ignorant of all the information that is now available, about everything under the sun, but we are convinced that it is by the manipulation of this information that our societies appear to operate and be managed. Feeling ignorant, we are fearful; feeling afraid, we are angry.

We then turn this Wrath against "The System," or whatever we like to call it, which we believe is the possessor of the knowledge that we do not have and cannot master, and the possessor in particular of the clues to that knowledge that we think gives it power over our lives, and would in turn give us power over our own lives if only we possessed it. Whenever people have directed their Wrath against "The System" in recent years, or some similar abstraction such as "The Establishment," it has been less against its power as such than against the information that is supposed to be the source of that power. It is our fear of this vast body of information, unknown and unknowable to us, that makes us think that all power has become a conspiracy, not only all power, but all authority that otherwise should be given our respect; we turn our Anger against them.

In much of the propaganda and mythology of our times, there lies this belief that, if only we attain mastery of that knowledge and the clues to decoding it, we will attain mastery also of our own lives, and this belief is also in part responsible for our misleading concept of individual and human rights. Give us the key to the bank where the knowledge is stored, and lo and behold! we will all at last be free. The concept of rights as it has developed includes the notion that there is something outside ourselves that has only to be made accessible to us, for us at once to achieve the capacities and even the natures to which we aspire. The individual is defined by his or her power, and the extent of that power by the extent of his or her knowledge; when that liberating knowledge is supposedly denied, one of the subtlest prescriptions for Anger has been filled.

The example may seem trivial, but consider the student whose professor has given him an "F" for an incompetent performance. He will not, these days, be angry at himself; the idea that his own incapacity or slovenliness is to blame, if it enters his mind at all, will at once be dismissed; and he will not just be angry for a moment at his professor, uttering an expletive that is not meant to be serious. He will discover the resources of Wrath and direct it against "The System" that makes such demands on him. It is the course of studies that is at fault. If it is philosophy he is studying, he should not have to begin with Heraclitus. Who's Heraclitus, man? What does he have to say to the twentieth century? If he cannot write a paragraph of coherent prose, he should not be given a low grade for so insignificant a failing. The ejaculation of a few monosyllables should score as much. It's real, man. So he will ask to choose for himself what he should study, to decide how he should be taught, and even to determine which professors are fit to be his instructors. All of which has happened in recent years. This is Wrath, even though it may seem to be so passive and banal, fury given license.

It is related to Envy, but it is not the same. The hatred of Wrath is even more destructive than the morose regret of Envy. Envy bites its nails. Wrath scratches and tears with them. The students who destroyed the lifetime's work of a scholar by burning his notes or tore up the card catalog of a library, were not envious of the knowledge that they did not possess, fearing that their lack of it demeaned them. They were fearful of its power, which they were not prepared to make any serious effort to attain. For it is worth dwelling on this image from what has actually happened in our time. Burning the notes of a scholar, tearing up the card catalog of a library, destroying things that are so mutely unoffending: This is not just a freakish way of behaving, about which we need only be idly curious, but the venting of Wrath, bitter-hearted and with malice aforethought, hating and determined on vengeance, with no check on its savagery, and having no concern for the fitness of its actions, from which the victim suffers far more pain and loss than any momentary satisfaction that his torturer enjoys.

Envy has no need to rationalize its biliousness. The object of its resentment is always a person, studied so long that every lineament is known. But in order to invent an enemy, when in fact there is none, Wrath must rationalize. The scholar and his notes are inoffensive— not even Anger can pretend that he is the enemy—so he has to be presented as something other than a scholar. He is the representative of "The System" or whatever, and few things are more characteristic of our age, and few things are more idly tolerated, than the way in which Anger is turned so often on abstractions, which are then personified in actual people, who may therefore be justly persecuted at one's own willing. If one searches the rationalizations for their excuses, one will find that behind them there always lies the belief, almost the superstition, that somewhere is a body of knowledge that is inaccessible and menacing.

It is partly for this reason that Wrath turns naturally to conspiracy theories, which are again peculiarly a mark of our times. There in the conspiracy—unproved maybe but its existence believed—is the most durable of enemies. Even if he does not exist, he can be said to exist, in the dark and hidden from us. The fact that we cannot see him is proof only of his cunning, and above all it is proof of his control over the knowledge that is kept from us, since he conceals the knowledge even of his conspiracy. Even in our everyday flashes of Anger, we reach to the idea of conspiracy. However slight the original provocation, we accuse the other of trying to get at us, to undermine us, to go behind our backs, until at last we cry in triumph, "I know what you're up to." Wrath will always discover a plot, and the existence of this plot, however imaginary, is the most all-encompassing of its justifications. A simple explanation will never do. The socks were never mislaid by accident, or even merely by a little carelessness, they were mislaid by intention, and probably the other plotted to mislay them. Wrath needs its enemy, it will create its enemy, it then nourishes its enemy.

The conspirator is solitary. We think of him in his cell, at best in a cellar. But the person who is always imagining conspiracies is no less solitary. He also is cut off from the real world and looks out instead on a world of enemies. Conspiracy theories are as furious obsessions as conspiracies themselves. Their authors are like recluses; their rooms are no less like cells, with evidence only of their one preoccupation; they are wrapped up in documents. Their method is mainly exegesis. From a few texts, which they pore over endlessly, they produce their interpretations; they go on adding more footnotes, year by year, but rarely more substance. The world as it is, with all its accident and waywardness, is blocked from their view. They are angry men in a world of their own, which they have peopled with angry men; and again one must emphasize that what makes them angry is the belief, nagging at them, that there is a body of information that gives power to those who control it.

If we are to understand this fear of ignorance, as a source of our Wrath, we must look at it in another of its forms, one that torments us perhaps more than any other. We fear our ignorance of ourselves, because we have been taught that we may acquire a full self-knowledge, not by the effort of a lifetime, an effort that anyhow is doomed to failure even though we are bound to make it, but by the perusal of a few manuals, now and then with the guidance of a psychiatrist, and by gazing fondly on ourselves with an idle but flattering curiosity. We are incited to rake over our feelings, examine our motives and desires (where they are most easily accessible to us on the surface) to make sure that they are true, and then to explain to others how true they are. We go on and on at each other, with our self-inquiries and revelations, which, if they were really deep, we could not confess so freely, until we come up with the cunning reassurance, "I'm OK, you're OK." People today spend interminable hours telling each other "where they're coming from," and "where they're at," when all that they are doing is inventing implausible little fictions about themselves and their lives. Every new relationship is begun with the dubious exchange of these quirkly little maps.

Reduced to this condition of mutual self-deception, our relationships become a kind of mutual therapy. An intimate relationship is satisfactory only if it satisfies "who I am"—which means only "who I *think* or *feel* I am"—at any moment at which one chooses to raise the banner of one's self. Not only can one know oneself and so be sure what one wants, but the other should know the same things about one and be constantly alert to one's pleas for a reassuring massage. Thus the fires of Wrath are stoked. The relationship is reduced to an almost political battle over each other's claimed rights to be gratified as a "person." There is no mutuality to be cared for, only two individualities, each with its demands for itself in the moment. The fallacies are those which we are examining. We assume that there is a kind of knowledge, in this case of ourselves, that we may easily attain, and by which we can define ourselves, and so acquire a complete mastery over our own lives, including the ability to command happiness at will. When this proves to be false, fear and frustration enter to do their work, and again the groundwork for Anger is laid. From this assumed knowledge of ourselves, we argue that any felt need or desire or longing represents a right that must be granted, and when satisfaction is not forthcoming, our resentments work in as deadly a manner in our private as in our public lives. We know what we want, and it must be granted; it is a right, even in love.

In all the examples that have been given, one incitement is common. People have been taught to believe that human knowledge is a box of tricks, which they have only to open to draw on it for what they want, so to make all well for themselves or their class or for the world. There is of course no such box, but when they believe that access to it is being arbitrarily denied to them, or discover that the tricks do not work, they are consumed with Wrath at their impotence. For they are being denied the greatest of supposed rights, the right to complete control over their own lives, and to make of them whatever they choose to think they are or can be. Wrath is particularly a sin of impotence as in the tantrum of the child whose wishes are crossed, and we are today made to feel impotent by the false expectations that are aroused in us, especially of the imagined potentialities that lie unjustly oppressed in us.

Merely by demonstrating some of the forms that Anger takes in our age, we have illustrated the theological definition of anger as an example of perverted love. It is the love of justice perverted into the desire for revenge and for the injury of someone else; justice is the proclaimed motive of every manifestation of Wrath at which we have looked. The motive in some cases may be genuine; there are injustices to be put right. But the love of justice is again and again turned into the hatred of someone. Whenever love is translated into hatred, we know that sin has entered and wreaked its havoc. Our societies are to some extent to blame. They are so organized that they increase the feeling of impotence, and therefore of frustration, which is yet another of the most common provocations to Wrath. This is not only, and perhaps not even primarily, because they are so large and impersonal that people are bound to feel impotent and frustrated, their Anger ready to burst out and as likely as not to splatter some innocent bystanders in our life. People do not merely feel harassed by it. They also begin to feel, as they rush hither and thither, trying to do all the things that their societies bid and entice them to do, that they cannot ever accomplish them all, and their feeling of inadequacy turns easily into frustration and fear and Anger.

But our Wrath is a sin of our age, rather than of our societies. Theology has always recognized that one of the forms that Anger takes is impatience with oneself and at one's own faults. "Others again become indignant and highly impatient when they observe their own imperfection," says St. John of the Cross. "And this great impatience derives from their ambition to become saints in a single day. Many of them have good intentions and make grand resolutions, but they are not humble and place too much confidence in themselves. And the more resolutions they make, the more often they fall and the greater becomes their annoyance with themselves." This is deeply what we have been describing. People feverishly add to the already increased tempo of life, by expecting that they should and can do many things. They whip up their own feelings of impotence; and all the time their societies egg them on to try more, to fulfill themselves a hundredfold again in yet other ways.

Our societies find it difficult to subdue the Wrath of our age, and especially to repel the idea that any felt want may be claimed as a right, because we have erected an exaggerated concept of the individual and of his capacity to find an ultimate fulfillment only in himself. We are left stranded between the wider society, in which we are no longer able or even invited to participate from day to day with any real meaning, and the mere pinpoints of ourselves, for which anyhow only the thinnest gruel is provided as nourishment. It is no wonder that the individual turns round angrily and says that there must be more to life than this, and that it must immediately be given as a right. "Bullshit!" people shout in their Wrath at superior authority. "Bullshit!" they shout at superior knowledge. "Bullshit!" they shout at traditional values. "Bullshit!" they shout at whatever seems to get in their way, for it is these that must be the cause of their inadequacy. One of the consequences of Anger that is condemned is the habit of foul language and blasphemy: We have only to listen with our ears to hear the Wrath of our age everywhere.

CHAPTER FOUR
SLOTH or ACEDIA

SLOTH OR ACEDIA

BY SLOTH IN our everyday idiom we mean only idleness, and idleness can be attractive, even something that is worth cultivating. Lovers will laze by the bank of a river. Few pleasures are greater than lingering over a lunch or a drink with a friend. Simply to idle away the day—how better sometimes to spend one? To stroll, to window shop, to saunter, to have no particular purpose in mind, not to hurry, not to fret, not to make an effort! "What is this life if, full of care, / We have no time to stand and stare?" asked W.H. Davies, and there can be only one answer: It is not worth the living. But we would not say that any of these are slothful. They might even be described, if it did not spoil the idea of them, as forms of activity. The mark of them all is that they are done for the love of doing them.

But the sin of Sloth is a state of dejection that gives rise to torpor of mind and feeling and spirit; to a sluggishness or, as it has been put, a poisoning of the will; to despair, faintheartedness, and even desirelessness, a lack of real desire for anything, even for what is good. Sloth is a deadly sin because it is "an oppressive sorrow that so weighs upon a man's mind that he wants not to exercise any virtue." It can even sorrow in the divine good instead of rejoicing in it. In pathology, sloth means a morbid inertia and, by transference, it means the same spiritually. In all of these aspects it is peculiarly an affliction of our time, much more prevalent than it seemed to the medieval theologian. W. H. Auden called ours the "age of anxiety." Anxiety in this sense is modern—one Protestant theologian has said that it is post-Reformation—and it is not unrelated to Sloth.

Our popular speech is today full of phrases that suggest an indifference and apathy that amount to spiritual and emotional torpor. Hang loose! Laid back! I can dig that, man! Play it cool! Go with the flow! That's heavy! Don't get uptight! There is Sloth in all of them, and they have their counterpart in more traditional phrases. I couldn't care less! I don't give a damn! What's that to me? I mind my own business! Live and let live! Nothing is worth getting very serious about, except one's own wants at the moment in one's own immediate environment. I'm OK, you're OK. So what reason is there to worry? "In the world it is called Tolerance, but in hell it is called Despair," says Dorothy Sayers. "It is the sin that believes in nothing, cares for nothing, seeks to know nothing, interferes with nothing, enjoys nothing, hates nothing, finds purpose in nothing, lives for nothing, and remains alive because there is nothing for which it will die." As each generation in the modern age has followed deeper in the footprints of its predecessors, this description has applied to it with continually more accuracy and force. There is not a trumpet note in our lives to call us to our feet.

Most of the recipes of the "human potential" movement for personal relationships and "self-actualization" are prescriptions for emotional and spiritual Sloth. Life is reduced by them to merely Passages from meaningless "now" to meaningless "now," each to be negotiated with just enough precautionary effort to avoid all but the slightest difficulty and pain. Our lives are made into a succession of episodes, in which any fulfillment or happiness will be largely an accident, at best a coincidence, and in either case will be of little account to us or to anyone else. In fact, we can give only the barest account of them, for there are to be no narratives to our lives, no intelligible threads running through them; at the same time they are stripped of all but the most slender association with the narratives of our societies, since we are persuaded to live apart from them in the little oases of our selves. Such are the "human potential" and "self-actualization" that are recommended: lives that have no personal history—only a succession of masks fitted to ever changing roles—lived amid an environment that has been denuded of human history. Pied pipers have only to pipe today, and adults as well as children dance after them into a total vacuity.

The name for such a condition is Sloth, and perhaps what is most dispiriting about our time is, not merely that we are persuaded that this is how we should be, but that the voices raised against it are so weak and timid. Schoolteachers themselves have become slothful. They have abandoned the painful task of combating the natural idleness of their pupils and instead let their little victims play at what they will, and what they will is of course applauded as their self-actualization. From cradle to grave, life is to be avoided by therapies, even when they are disguised as something else. We should think hard why the phrase "learning experience" has been found necessary. By learning we mean something is learned. When we say "I learned this today," there is a measure by which to test its accuracy and value. "What has been learned," something objective outside ourselves, is what counts. But when we say "That was a great learning experience I had today," we mean only a rather vague and superficial response in ourselves, in which what happened to us is more important than anything else. We are talking merely of a subjective feeling, which makes us feel good, a form of self-indulgence and self-entertainment. We are turned in, to delight in our own experiencing, rather than out, to the obstinate fact of something other.

We can put beside our own weak prescriptions one that is stronger, with a strong prescription. "I cannot answer the question, 'Who am I?' except in terms of some sort of statement of the plans and purposes of my life," said Josiah Royce seventy years ago in *The Philosophy of Loyalty*. "I should say that a person, an individual self, may be defined as a human life lived according to a plan . . . He acknowledged that "every man inevitably finds himself as apparently occupying the centre of his own universe. . . . Yes, the entire and infinite visible world, to be even more exact, seems to each of you to have its centre about where the bridge of your nose happens to be." As such individuals, we seek happiness. "Happiness involves the satisfaction of desires," but our "natural desires are countless and conflicting. What satisfies one desire defeats another." We therefore need to be enabled to choose between them—to learn to know our own will, and how to exercise it—and for this we need a plan and purpose. But where and how can we find them? Inside ourselves, the voice of our age insinuates. Royce disagreed.

"Since no man can find a plan of life by merely looking within his own chaotic nature, he has to look without, to the world of conventions, deeds and causes. . . . Only a cause, then, an absorbing and fascinating social cause, which by his own will and consent comes to take possession of his life . . . only such a cause, dignified by the social unity that it gives to many individual lives, but rendered also vital for the loyal man by the personal affection which it awakens in his heart, only such a cause can unify his outer and inner world." And he invokes us in his conclusion: "Seek, then, serenity, but let it be the serenity of the devotedly and socially active being. Otherwise your spiritual peace is a mere feeling of repose, and, as such, contents at its best but one side of your natures, namely, the more sensuous side."

Royce had not read the literature of "human potential" and "self-actualization," but portents of it were in the air, and he had a strong inkling of what must come. "A mere feeling of repose . . . but one side of your nature . . . the more sensuous side"—these phrases do not only summarize where we have arrived, seventy years later, they are more and more what our societies choose to celebrate. "I do my thing and you do your thing," runs what Donald Heinz has called "the misty-eyed Gestalt prayer" of Fritz Perls. "You are you and I am I, and if by chance we find each other, it's beautiful." This is the extent of the human potential we are to actualize, the depth of our awareness of ourselves and of the others whom by chance we find. It is Sloth as a way of life. All that is to be explored, all that is to be guarded, is a mere fraction of oneself, in contact with a mere fraction of others, in a world limited to the narrowest concerns.

One does not have to adopt Royce's idealistic philosophy in order to recognize that he was, in his own day, setting himself against a false concept of individualism that has continued to dominate our century, at least in our societies. The most monstrous of its falsehoods is the belief that the individual can find fulfillment and salvation in nothing but his or her own self, and the denial that we are members one of another, and that "the solidarity of mankind links the crimes of each to the sorrows of all." This form of individualism rests ultimately on complacency. It is the complacency of the comfortable, as they have grown in number, and we have only to look around us in our affluent societies to see how deeply it has taken root. One can even hear denials that we are our brother's keeper. This complacency is again our Sloth.

We must confront it unforgivingly, because it is causing havoc in our societies and therefore in our personal lives. It is the individualism of the bourgeois, given the same rationalizations as before, but with a twist that was unpredictable. Its first commandment is, now as before, that we should "look out for Number 1." (It is interesting that many who proclaim this commandment are nevertheless embarrassed by it and talk archly of

"Numero Uno" as if to say that they do not really mean it.) The twist that has followed is the result of our affluence. The bourgeois two generations ago—say, Babbit—still needed some of the institutions of society, so he took their morality as his own, and willingly and with his consent gave at least his outward loyalty to them and to what they preached. It is true that their morality had become little more than a series of prohibitions, and that Babbit's adherence to it was without any real understanding or conviction, that there was even a restlessness in his adherence that was a portent of revolt. All the same, the allegiance was given. But in an age of plenty, the bourgeois need not acknowledge even these obligations, or the institutions embodying them, because he believes that he can afford to live without them.

"Looking out for Number 1" has been given the formidable reinforcement that one can today live entirely by, with, and for oneself, and even *to* oneself, since it is seldom anyone but oneself whom one is addressing. "I am I, you are you" or "I'm OK, you're OK" are profoundly self-centered and self-indulgent statements, which in effect tell the "you"—the Other—to get on by itself and leave one to get on by oneself. Fifty years ago, Walter Lippmann said of the Babbits, "they are ungoverned and yet unfree," and if we look now at the grandchildren of Babbit, his words ring yet more true. "They are creatures of the passing moment who are vaguely unhappy in a boring and senseless existence," he went on, and today we might say the same, except that they are not even vaguely unhappy, but vaguely persuaded that they are in fact doing what they want and being what they wish. All of these are descriptions of Sloth.

Peter Viereck once drew a portrait of the son of Babbit, whom he saw about him in the 1950s, acidly calling him Gaylord Babbit. In the quarter of a century that has elapsed, as the grandchildren of Babbit have grown up, the slide away from any idea of personal guilt, or of gravity in pursuing some purpose in one's life, of commitment to someone or something other than oneself, of sacrificing even one's peace of mind to that purpose, has continued at a speed that even then could not be foreseen. If one returns now to Babbit, he seems a more understandable character than before, if not more sympathetic. Many of his arguments with his children were between one generation that had known when money kept its value and another generation that sensed that the value of money had been undermined forever. Babbit himself sensed this, which is one reason why he sputtered and declaimed. Many of his defenses of his positions now seem tragic rather than pathetic, because he felt that they had been undermined in their very citadel, as he believed it to be, by the first taste of indiscriminate plenty and by the first geological fault in society that was caused by permanently inflationary pressures. How to preach the virtue of thrift, say, to those who know it will earn no reward? How also to preach against the vices of Sloth to those to whom plenty is readily at hand?

There is now no "we" in our vocabularies. "We" is precluded from statements like "I am I, you are you." It is impossible to translate "I'm OK, you're OK" into the plural. It deliberately does not say "We're OK," or claim to say it, because "we" as a unit does not command our allegiance, only separate identities in transaction with each other. In this way even the family is no longer a "we" but an exercise in mutual therapy for the self-centered egos of its members. If any of the members, parent or child, finds that the therapy is insufficient, that it wants more massage, it is free to leave, because the affluence of our societies will, in one way or another, support it in this choice. Jonathan Livingston Seagull was again the sentimental idealization of this grossly distorted individualism. But the very effortlessness of the freedom that he was supposed to enjoy was a symbol of Sloth. For what we are talking about is a condition in which it is becoming inconceivable that most people will surrender themselves, willingly and with their own consent, to some cause or calling or to someone else on which or on whom they set a value beyond their own selfish gratification.

We may say this of the face of Sloth: that at any age it is the face of those who are already old beyond their years, who seem never to have known any springtime, whether in their own lives or around them each year, in whom the sap seems never to have risen. ("The sap of life does not reach them," Lippmann said of the Babbits, "their taproots having been cut.") Even in those who should be reaching the May Day of their lives, if Sloth has taken root, their eyes are already downcast with their own emptiness of spirit, their mouth is already slack with lack of purpose either to speak or to embrace, and in their flesh are already the intimations of fold upon fold of the worldweariness that they seem to have known since childhood. When we come to speak of the forms that Lust takes in our time, we will find that Sloth is deeply ingrained in many of them, and especially in the refusal to get deeply involved in a relationship with anyone. It is when Jonathan Livingston Seagull ends his first giddy flight by falling into the void of a singles bar that one sees how early Sloth can wreak its damage in a dejection of the body and mind and spirit.

The picture is overdrawn, it may be said. It will seem overdrawn only if it is thought that Sloth cannot often take the form of what Dorthy Sayers said was one of its favorite tricks, "to dissemble itself under the cover of a whiffling activity of the body." The recent popularity of outdoor sports—on the tennis court or the golf course, carrying surfboards to the sea and then carrying them back again, marathon running or even just jogging, and a score more that are now pursued with zealotry—is evidence of a society whose members imagine that they are being strenuous when they are only engaging in a whiffling activity of the body. There is nothing against such activities in themselves. There is everything against the celebration of them as some kind of strenuous spirituality. When runners or joggers say that they experience a "high"—a characteristic word of our time—they are talking precisely of a whiffling sensation. A high is whiffling by nature, to be enjoyed as such if that is one's taste, but hardly to be regarded as an encounter with truth. To improve one's tennis is to improve one's tennis. It is not to improve one's soul, even if one has called Zen to one's aid.

At this point we have arrived in California, "the state of fulfillment" as it may be called, where the "Spoiled Child of the Western World" has come to rest. And one means, to rest. It is there that the human potential movement, as Cyril McFadden has nicely put it, "takes the place of other light industries," there that being "laid back" and "mellowing out" are day-long preoccupations, accompanied by the chatter of a self-congratulatory and undisturbing concern with "life goals," there that body language is most generally assumed to be a superior alternative to verbal language. And there also is the greatest concentration of institutes and retreats for self-actualization, whether by "transactional analysis or Transcendental Meditation, bioenergetics or biofeedback, Scientology or Silva Mind Control, nude marathons or primal screaming, psychosynthesis or Creative Consciousness, Rolfing or the Feldenkrais Method, yoga or lomi body work," not to mention est or a challenger to it known as Actualizations. The list is taken from a California journalist, who says of Actualizations that it works miracles on people through "awareness workshops" that last only four days, which is a short road to heaven.

There is Sloth in the motives of all of them: an excessive interest in and love of one's self and a deficient interest in and love of other people. But there is Sloth also in the methods. In spite of the apparent emphasis in some of them on self-development disciplines, the self-examination and self-correction that are demanded are paltry. The promise in the title of Adelaide Bry's book, *est: 60 Hours That Transform Your Life*, is much the promise of them all, give or take an hour or two. What they provide is the opportunity to explore yet again the condition of one's ego, under a greater or lesser pretense that one is bent on one's self-improvement. There may be many reasons why these gurus and charlatans thrive more in California than elsewhere, but it is hard not to think that it is merely a forerunner of what our societies are to be, in which a life of material well-being must be represented as one of immaterial blessedness and, with hedonism elevated to a spiritual exercise, it can be claimed that the union of body and spirit is at last achieved.

If you are driving along Route 1, the Pacific Coast Highway, in a convertible with the top down, with the surf breaking on the beaches to your left, with the mountains spilling down to the road on your right, with the brilliant sun in a blue sky, with a woman by your side, with a dreamy voice on your car radio singing "You are the honeysuckle, I am the bee," what can be of much concern, except one's own self-actualization? This is only the individualism of our age that has undergone a sea change under the palm trees. The sociologist James Q. Wilson, who was brought up in Southern California, has said of those who went there earlier in this century: "The people had no identities except their personal identities. The absence of such group identities and of neighborhoods associated with those identities may be one reason for the enormous emphasis on 'personality'. . . . Everybody was compared in terms of his or her personality . . . To be 'popular' and 'sincere' was vital."

But all of this was noticed almost a hundred years ago by Josiah Royce, who was born in California a mere six years after his parents journeyed there during the Gold Rush, and who wrote what is still the one classic book about the state. He described the program for the Bear Flag Republic in 1846 as "A government whose subjects were free to do just as they liked. . . . In short, a government of general good humor." He found in California, even while he loved it, "an extravagant trust in luck, a previously unknown blindness to social duties, . . . a long-continued career of social apathy, of treasonable public carelessness. . . . In short, the Californian has too often come to love the mere fulness of life and to lack reverence for the relations of life." There the individual struggles "to escape, like a fool, from his moral obligations to society." In a pungent phrase, he found in it "a sort of irreligious liberty." However obviously this is true of California then and now, its interest to us here is that it points where all our societies seem to be going.

Actualizations has no money-back guarantee, says its founder Stewart Emery. "It does, however, have what Stewart calls 'a shit-back guarantee.' Anyone who gets tired of being happy, who doesn't want to go on actualizing, can have his 'shit' back—his 'stuff.'" He can revert to what he was before his four days at $250, "with all of its bad memories of the past and dread expectations of the future." The triviality of what is being offered in the name of "happiness" could hardly be better expressed. Sloth has been described in theology as a "hatred of all spiritual things which entail effort," and "faintheartedness in matters of difficulty" in striving for perfection. It will "endure no hardship nor any penance," says the Parson in his tale. All of this slackness and self-excusing, slovenliness and lack of endeavor, one finds in today's prescriptions for feeling good about oneself. But the "shit" of which we are so easily relieved is in fact needed if we are to try to do well.

We should not be surprised that once again it is put best by St. John of the Cross: "As to spiritual Sloth, many beginners shy away and flee from things of a spiritual nature because they do not appeal to their sensible taste. For, as they have found much sweetness in spiritual things, they are wearied by things in which they find no such sweetness. Since they want to have completely their own way in spiritual things and insist on following the inclination of their will, it is with a dejected spirit and with great repugnance that they enter upon the narrow way, which as Christ says, is the way of life." He says that too many people are moved to indulge in spiritual exercises and devotional practices by the consolation and pleasure they find in them, and the more we look at the pathetic little orthodoxies that attract us today, the more we find that they are no more than balms to sweeten our self-love.

We will not come to grips with the fact of evil, but we also exaggerate its power to excuse us from endeavor. Behind our Sloth there lie a series of rationalizations, of which one of the most alluring and destructive is the belief, which our culture has inculcated in us, that the evil of the world and of our societies is so great that there is little that we can do to combat it. The evil, it must be noticed, is out there, not in ourselves; and out there it is so all-encompassing, so certain to bring everything to destruction and death, so without hope of any redemption, that we may excuse ourselves from any fruitless concern to combat it, any trifling acknowledgment that our own evil contributes to it, any foolish effort to reduce or contain or overcome it. We retreat instead into our own private pursuits, persuaded that at least in them the half-hearted efforts of our spineless love will be enough to get by, the love that we have made spineless by our own trivialization of it by centering it on ourselves.

The world is evil, filled with destruction. Creation is evil, condemning us to die. Life is an absurdity, since we all end under ground. The evil of our societies, embedded in institutions so big that we cannot hope to control them, is beyond our concern or correction. So we will retreat to our oases, and cultivate our Sloth. We have doubly armed it, for nothing is redeemable but ourselves; there is health in us, if we massage ourselves enough, but in nothing else, in nothing of which we are part. The excuse for Sloth is complete. To say that our societies sin is not the same as saying that they are beyond redemption. How much greater a fault it is for us to look upon the wonder and goodness of creation and be obsessed by the fact that we decay in it and some day must leave it. So we whiffle away our lives, with no real purpose or strenuousness. Who's for tennis? In at least its courts, we will serve. We will ride to paradise on a golf cart.

But Sloth has not done with its exemptions. By exaggerating the evil and futility of everything but ourselves, we pretend to an innocence that has no justification in fact, that again stirs us to no strenuousness of endeavor. Such evil as there is in us is society's doing and, in so far as it troubles us at all, we may exorcise it by our therapies. Almost all the recipes of the "human potential" movement offer only appeasements. We use transcendental meditation as we once used coffee breaks. We gather in groups that have no other life than themselves, no association with any other parts of our lives, no other purpose but to give us a benevolent endorsement. They ask very little of us except that we should ask little of ourselves. We reduce our desires to the shallowest of levels, so that we can then persuade ourselves that we have satisfied them. One of the most beguiling of temptations, as Spinoza said, is to entertain desires for only part of our natures, and for only the present and not the future. Our wishes for ourselves are now so trivial and fixed on the present, that we have in fact reached the condition of desirelessness that is Sloth.

At the root of it all, in the language of theology, is despair of the mercy of God, and therefore a despair also of his creation. There is in it an almost Manichean belief that matter and flesh fall into the realm of darkness, but of course without the Manichean prescription for leading an ascetic life. Even in secular terms it is a refusal to be moved, and to be moved especially to any real endeavor, by the contemplation of the good and the beautiful. Our art and our literature today do not teach us how to praise and rejoice. There is an emphasis on what is ugly and corrupt and harsh, which is just as sentimental as if everything is presented as lovely and innocent and benign. It leads to either disillusionment or escapism, even to escapism as a flight from disillusion. What is not given its proper weight is reality. G.K. Chesterton said that St. Thomas Aquinas, when he was troubled by doubt, chose to believe in more reality and not in less. There are moments in all our lives when it seems the hardest of prescriptions, and there are some eras more than others that seem to find it particularly hard. Yet as we will see in the last of these essays, it is this attention to reality that we need to call us back from our Sloth. We will not become passionate and devout in our lives as long as we are merely "knowing" about the world.

Anxiety is a close companion of fear, but whereas fear is always a fear of something, as has often been pointed out, anxiety is essentially a dread of nothing. This is one of the themes of our "age of anxiety," but, however much there may be in the conditions of our time to incite this dread, we must recognize that we are capable of manufacturing it in ourselves. Kierkegaard at least always wondered if he might not be responsible for his own melancholy. "And was not this sickness hard enough for me to bear in time, that I not only should suffer but become guilty through it?" he asks. "The deformed man has after all only to bear the pain of being deformed, but how dreadful if being deformed made him guilty!" This completely sincere man was never quite sure of the character and significance of his "monstrous melancholy," as he called it, even as he struggled with anguish, until his lonely death, against "the pale, bloodless, hard-lived, midnight shapes," to whom he himself, he was not afraid to say, gave their life. He asked himself again and again "whether in my religious feeling there is not a certain pleasure in self-torture."

Kierkegaard's driving down to find the roots of his melancholy, to be clear at long last about its religious, poetic, or romantic value, bears some comparison with the courage of Freud in his own prolonged self-analysis. To trivialize it by imitating it, without any of the anguish, is a characteristic sin of our time. Especially in the late 1960s, one could stand at the check-out counters in college book stores and watch the students pay for *Fear and Trembling* or *The Sickness Unto Death* or *The Concept of Dread* with their credit cards and put them in their backpacks. One does not know how far they got with them. But what they were looking for was a "trip," and they reminded one of Kierkegaard's own remark, "Who in modern times has been so much used by parsons and professors as Pascal? His ideas are appropriated— but Pascal's asceticism and his hair-shirt are omitted." The one thing for which Kierkegaard did not use his *dementia,* as he called it, was as a justification for the dejection of Sloth. He may have had a morbid constitution, and suffered from a manic-depressive psychosis, as psychiatrists have held. He had a phobia for the sun and barricaded his windows. His fear of fire was hysterical and, sweating and trembling, he took frantic precautions against it. There was his mania for sprinkling eau-de-cologne on the stove before working, and his collection of cups from which a fresh pair had to be chosen every day. But he never used any of it for the self-excusing for which his ideas are used today.

Sloth is eating at us, devouring all inclination to continue the human endeavor at even the level that has been sustained in the past. For we are reaching the stage at which we will no longer regard ourselves as part of that endeavor. We barely know our civilization any more. We do not read the ancients. Even the classics of our own literature are becoming closed books to us. We make little or no effort to understand our science, with the instructions that it has to give and the wonders it has to show. We allow no authority to the past and entertain no obligation to the future. We do not observe the rules of grammar or syntax. We disdain our dictionaries and let our vocabulary grow slack. We seem to think that we may communicate without bothering to speak accurately to each other, and even without speaking with the complexity and discrimination of language at all. We will rely on touch and feel; and the human race will end its long trek across the centuries, it sometimes seems we are bent on proving, as a speechless race of touchy-feelies. We even think that we can think without troubling to think. And yet we look surprised and hurt if we are accused of being slothful.

Children are too idle to obey. Parents are too sluggish to command. Pupils are too lazy to work. Teachers are too indolent to teach. Priests are too slack to believe. Prophets are too morbid to inspire. Men are too indifferent to be men. Women are too heedless to be women. Doctors are too careless to care well. Shoemakers are too slipshod to make good shoes. Writers are too inert to write well. Street cleaners are too bored to clean streets. Shop clerks are too uninterested to be courteous. Painters are too feckless to make pictures. Poets are too lazy to be exact. Philosophers are too fainthearted to make philosophies. Believers are too dejected to bear witness. This may seem too sweeping a judgment; there are of course individual exceptions to this general apathy. But before we dismiss it as too sweeping, we must ask then why our societies have to spend so much time trying to correct us.

In schools and then at work and in the course of our day-to-day lives, there are a score of devices to try to "motivate" us. The prescriptions for "self-improvement" are themselves a part of this attempt to supply us with motivation. These artificial recipes would not be necessary if it was not recognized that we are now generally slothful in the ways that have been described here. Our societies reduce us to a slothful interest in ourselves and then have to find ways of trying to make us attend to our social duties. Once again one can see that it is the relationship of the individual with his society that today lies at the core of our troubles. One of the corrections of Sloth is *fortitudo*, which is perhaps best translated as *the strength of courage*. Such an ideal for the citizen would have been understood in almost any other age but our own. Our societies simply do not ask this strength of courage from us, or even much force of character, and so have held out carrots, to make us do sullenly what we ought to do with devotion.

For one has only to think about it and one realizes that Sloth is preeminently a sin of omission. To put it more positively, it is a sin of neglect. We neglect what we ought to do, and especially we neglect our neighbors. This neglect may amount even to callousness. We pass by on the other side, partly out of Pride, of which there is a lot in Sloth, but partly out of mere indolence, a laziness of the spirit as well of the flesh. Increasingly in our societies, we barely lift a finger for the poor and the downtrodden. Our technology and our gadgets have freed us from most drudgery, and what do we do with the time that is now available to us? We turn inward and become utterly absorbed in ourselves, and once again we see how all the sins, leashed together and pulling in harness at our inmost natures, drag us in the same direction.

We have made a religion of ourselves and, of all the sins, we have come nearest to making a religion of Sloth.

We seem actually to have faith in it. Mind one's own business, do not get involved. Live and let live, as we said at the beginning. In this way, we will not hurt, and not be hurt. Of course, the hurt is deep, both ways. It separates us from the rest of humanity, and so from our own humanity, just as in theological terms it separates us from God. There is no room for concern or caring in it. But in separating us from everything that is other than us, it separates from much of what is essentially us. Leaving us feckless, we become more feckless. And what is most terrible about it is that, even in our Sloth, we move across our landscape, like a cloud of locusts, devouring everything by doing nothing: seeing nothing, hearing nothing, telling nothing.

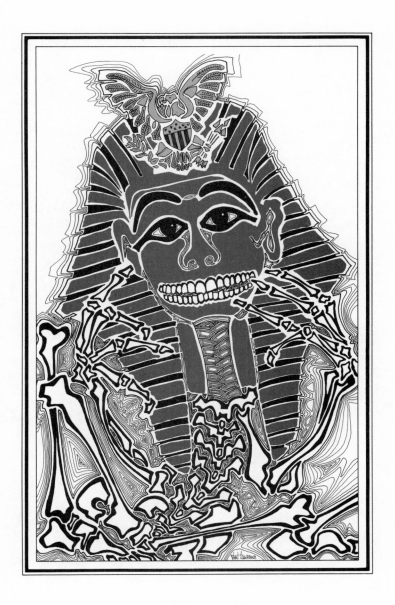

CHAPTER FIVE
AVARICE or AVARITIA

AVARICE or AVARITIA

WE THINK OF the miser, reaching his arms round the pile of coins on the table, until he embraces it, running his hands through them, and feeling the gold as it trickles through his fingers. So in at least one of its aspects we think of Avarice: niggardly and parsimonious. Shut away from life. "The unsunn'd heaps/Of miser's treasures," says Milton in *Comus*. If there are any windows where the miser counts his gold, they are shuttered, and before he enjoys the only thing he is able to enjoy, he bolts the door. It is not an accident that "miser" comes from the same root as "misery"—the Latin *miser*—or that the first meaning of "miserable" given in the dictionary is "stingy, miserly," and the first meaning of "miser" is "a wretched person." We think of Avarice as pinched and talk of penny-pinching. The life of the miser is pinched. Scrooge stays in our minds as the portrait of a miserable man, and not even the poorest man, though he may envy other rich men, will be found envying the impoverished existence to which the miser has reduced himself.

"Disquietude at the possible loss of wealth" is condemned as one of the consequences of Avarice, because it is a sign that the desire for wealth is prescribing one's life, narrowing its boundaries. The pile of gold on the table is a wall against the world. The miser hides behind it, and as his eyes are fixed on it, so are all his feelings. He can think of nothing else. He turns over his coins at night, and if he finds one that is brass, he cries out in pain and mortification. He may have a thousand more, but he cannot get this one coin out of his mind. He does not even use his wealth for pleasure. With all his hoard of gold, he makes only a poorhouse for himself. If all sin is a hardening of the heart against the fullness of life, no one's heart is more stringy than his.

When the miser fondles his gold, he makes an idol of it. He sets it up as a god. "Thou shalt not make unto thee any graven image," but that is exactly what he does. He gives a false value to his wealth and so places a mean value on himself. This is what Scrooge at last discovered: that it was his own nature that he was deforming. Idolatry is a form of self-abasement, before an object that is unworthy of such veneration. We talk of the Bitch Goddess Success, for example, because we give success a greater value than it deserves. We say correctly of some people that they idolize success, but our societies as a whole also worship it, and again the celebrity is a symbol. We do not applaud his talents, even if he should have any; we applaud his success. Since we have set him up as a graven image, the symbol of the success for which we are avaricious, we can as easily pull him down and set up another in his place. The emphasis that our societies place on success is one of the forms our Avarice now takes.

We must keep the miser in mind, but at the same time we have to admit that, at least at first sight, Avarice today does not seem to be shut away. On the contrary, our love of possessing seems to be out in the open, on view to everyone, even flaunted in their faces. ("If you have it, flaunt it," is a characteristic statement of our time, again a way of justifying any behavior.) Instead of just counting our money, we seem at least to be spending it, apparently for our enjoyment. The department stores get larger and larger each year and can hardly build fast enough to keep up with an insatiable appetite. Shopping malls spring up across the country almost overnight, some with floor space of more than two million square feet. A new Bloomingdale's is set down next to a new Saks Fifth Avenue, a new Saks Fifth Avenue next to a new Lord & Taylor. There is still business for them all. Neiman Marcus jumps from Dallas to Houston and then leaps to the East Coast to join the rest. Surely we are not miserly, when we spend so much. Surely we are not guilty of Avarice, when we throw away our money so freely. Scrooge gave nothing to anybody for Christmas, but we go on an orgy of spending. Are we not different, liberal with our money, liberated in our spending? But we are not different, unless it is that we are worse, that we cannot now even see our condition, or how in much of what we are today willing to applaud, it is Avarice that we are tolerating and condoning.

Avarice is, not so much the love of possessions, as the love merely of possessing. To buy what we do not need, more even than we need for our pleasure or entertainment, is a love of possessing for its own sake. We may think that we do not know any misers, since we do not come across people fondling their coins. But we all know people whose homes are so filled with possessions that there is scarcely room to turn in them. No one can need so many possessions or take any real pleasure in them. Our main impression in such houses is of distraction. Not only is our attention distracted by so many objects, so is the attention of their owner who should be acting as our host. His eyes dart around his room, noticing his possessions, and he must bring them to our notice. He must look constantly at what he owns, because it is the mere fact that he owns them that matters to him. He does not love his possessions for what they are—no one can love so many objects—he loves the fact that he is their possessor. He is, in short, a miser. He runs his eyes and his hands over them exactly as the miser does over his coins. He might as well live in a vault in a bank, with his treasures displayed around him, and let his friends visit him there on Tuesdays and Thursdays, between the hours of two and five p.m.

This difference between possessions and the mere

possessing needs underlining. The man who really loves the good wine he is serving, as he tastes it at his table, if he mentions it at all, will be heard to make only the briefest comment, almost to himself: "My, that's rather good, isn't it?" The wine is then left alone, to be itself and to be enjoyed by his guests. But there is another kind of man who praises the label. Even at his own table, he praises the label and asks his guests to praise it. He is not interested in the wine. It could hardly matter less to him. He is interested in the fact that he can afford the label. He is not even a "wine snob"; he is a "label snob." This is Avarice: the love of possessing, rather than the love of the possession. Whether it is true or not that "snob" is derived from *sine nobilitate*, this is in fact its first and real meaning: a vulgar person who is without nobility and therefore tries to emulate it. The snob is an emblematic figure of Avarice, wearing an Yves St. Laurent label on his shirt, exactly as he wears the label on his wine.

The most important fact about our shopping malls, as distinct from the ordinary shopping centers where we go for our groceries, is that we do not need most of what they sell, not even for our pleasure or entertainment, not really even for a sensation of luxury. Little in them is essential to our survival, our work, or our play, and the same is true of the boutiques that multiply on our streets. What we call our consumer societies may be gluttonous—and to that we will come—but they are ridden more subtly by Avarice. Our appetites are stimulated so that the product will be consumed, and thus we are incited to possess for the sake of possessing. We "must have that," when we see it, even though we do not need it. We buy more clothes than we need, more accessories (how revealing the word is) than we need, more furniture than we need, more bric-a-brac than we need, more *objets d'art* than we need, more cookbooks than we need, more kitchen equipment than we need, and even more gifts for our friends than they need. Even in the act of giving, we give what pleases the appetite for possessing, rather than what is meant to be a possession.

"For the man who has everything" has now been democratized and translated for the rest of us into "For people who need nothing." All of this is a distraction. We are out of our minds in our search for possessions. We scour the world for them. We spend hours in boutiques and department stores, wondering if we want something, whereas if we really needed or wanted it, we would have no doubts. What we today edify with the name of "design," from fashion to interior decoration, from a cooking pot to a candle, may have had some good intention and even some good effect. But it is first and last a worldwide enterprise of entrepreneurs, to persuade us to buy more than we need and to buy it more expensively than can be morally justified. Avarice is the inordinate love of temporal things, usually of riches, and it is inordinate "if one is not guided by a reasonable end in view." There is no reasonable purpose to much of our spending today, but our societies goad the Avarice that is already in us.

It might all seem trivial but harmless, until we consider what it does to us. We have all met people who have become their possessions, who do not possess but are possessed by them, and they seem to us to live in museums. They have been taken over by the objects around them, which seem more real than themselves. This may be most obvious in those who can afford to surround themselves with expensive and rare objects. But it is no less true of the suburban housewife who devotes her day to her possessions, cleans and polishes them and her house, more than any cleaning or polishing is necessary, because it is in them that she believes that she is on show and justified. She trusts them to speak for her more than herself, and in her attention to her family she often treats her husband and children as her possessions, showing them off also as evidence of herself. Whatever the excuses for her—and they may be many—her life is nevertheless ruled by Avarice.

For one thing that we are talking about is a middle-class way of life that derives its standards from the emulation of an upper middle-class way of life. When the bohemian revolted against the bourgeois in the last century, the most symbolic thing he did was discard the possessions of the bourgeois. (Sometimes he did not, it must be said, discard them for long. The spirit was weak, and the flesh was strong.) But the identification of the bourgeois with the *anxiety* to possess is correct. It is peculiarly his mark, and so the mark of his society; it is therefore the mark of our societies, which are bourgeois, and this anxiety is strangling us. Possessing for the sake of possessing is stifling, in us and in our societies, impulses that are more generous, more strenuous, and even more adventurous; it distracts those who might do more serious work, such as many of our artists and writers, into the avaricious pursuit of possessions that neither their work nor their lives in fact require, and in the end pervert and destroy.

If we now have no avant-garde in our art, standing against the more lackadaisical values of our societies, it is partly because the art market itself is built on the avaricious appetite of all those concerned in it: the Avarice of the dealer, the gallery owner, the art critic, the museum director, the artist of course, and not least the wealthy purchaser of art. Paintings hang on the walls of the rich as if they were certificates of stocks and bonds. It is all very well to look for intellectual or aesthetic reasons for the collapse of the avant-garde, the shallowness of much of contemporary art and literature, but we need also to think in terms sometimes of the most obvious motives, such as that too many of the people concerned with the making of art, not excluding the artist and the writer, have simply become too greedy to possess what they do not need.

The poor man does not have possessions, because he cannot afford them. The aristocrat does not need them, because his standing is assured without them. Neither of them has or needs possessions to establish or identify himself, in his own eyes or in those of others. A duke is still a duke, he still takes precedence, even when he is poor, and there have been many poor dukes. The true aristocrat may have a large and grand house, filled with rare and beautiful things, most of which he will have inherited, but he does not draw attention to them. They are even placed where one hardly notices them. One peers into a corner, and there is a Rubens. He almost pooh-poohs them. "Nice little thing," he will say of a treasure, and pass on to something else. He certainly does not count his possessions—he usually does not know what he has—for it is not they that elevate him. But if it is not the possession but the possessing of it that defines one's position, and even to some extent one's self, then the counting is necessary and is even the main purpose of the possessing, and this is generally the condition of any middle class, unless it is ruled by other values like the puritan middle-class of the last century.

Counting is the main pleasure of the miser, and counting is the main object of Avarice. "Money is the chief object of Avarice, not only because it provides for the control of many other objects, but because it offers the very simple satisfaction that it can be counted," says William F. May. The fact is that we have reached the stage at which most of the objects that we buy with our money have no real purpose but to be counted, even when we touch or look at them with the same pleasure as the miser at his gold. Every possession that is bought as a "status symbol" is bought primarily to be counted, and the status -symbol is peculiarly the brand of a middle-class society.

We depersonalize our own selves in our Avarice, in the objects that we use to represent and announce our status, and in the end we dehumanize ourselves. We begin to treat *ourselves* as objects. Among all the other objects by which we are surrounded, we become just one more object. A woman who has too many clothes, or who is hung with too much jewelry, seems to have become an object, and in fact we say so, calling her in the first case a clothes horse, and in the second a Christmas tree. It is not only others who may treat us as objects, we are accomplished at doing it ourselves. Those who surround themselves with things that they do not need, and do not even really want, soon cease to know what they do need or want; and in a little more time they cease also to know or be able to be themselves. Avarice leads to a form of self-annihilation.

Possessions in a modest degree, and acquired to a reasonable end, may be a legitimate pleasure: fitting and pleasing to ourselves and to others, as an expression of oneself and one's interests. We enjoy the evidence of our friends in their possessions, if it is genuinely the evidence of them, and their possessions do not come between them and us. We enjoy looking over someone's library or his collection of toy soldiers, if these are really his interests. But if the library is only of first editions or leather-bound editions that seem never to have been opened, or if the lead soldiers have been collected only because their price has risen on the antique market, then far from enjoying them we are put off by them. Some existentialists have set the "authentic order" of being far too severely against the "inauthentic order" of having. This is too rigid a dichotomy. Much that we are may be found in what we have. It is pleasant to see people with gardens they tend and know the houses they look after, but only if they never show them off as proof of their possessing. They must let us find them.

To strive for more possessions than one needs is, like

"being too solicitous in acquiring wealth," a sin that distracts and corrupts us at the center of our being. Avarice is high among the sins, and we cannot dismiss lightly the severity of Christ's words: "It is easier for a camel to go through the eye of a needle, than for a rich man to enter into the kingdom of God." Avarice makes us as unfit for salvation as that. Its hold is so strong that it is hard to combat it. "For though an avaricious man should, for the sake of avoiding death," says Spinoza, "cast his riches into the sea, he will nonetheless remain avaricious"; and for a rich man to divest himself of his wealth, to foundations or museums, cannot by itself save his soul. Even his divestiture is false; he still is not himself; he is still defined by his goods. His monument is to his money, not to himself. His fortune clings about his neck, even as he dies, and again it is worth remembering that a "fortune," meaning a large amount of money, is the same word as "fortune," meaning an accident of chance. It is only in the fifth definition of the word in *Webster's* that one comes to: "a condition in life as determined by material possessions." Following the four previous definitions— which concentrate on the elements of chance and fate— the word that matters in this fifth definition is "determined." If one is too rich, one is never really in charge of one's life; the possessing has taken over.

"Poor little rich girl" is not a sneer. It is a prayer for the rich. They are never free. They cannot get away from their possessions. There is very little that they can believe in others, because there is very little that they can believe in even themselves. They are never sure that they are behaving as they really would like to behave, because the apparent freedom of choice that their wealth gives them is a freedom they have not had to make themselves. It is not that their wealth makes life too easy, but that it makes it too difficult to find. This is why so many excessively rich people are recluses. There is nothing they can trust, because they cannot trust themselves. This pathetic quality of the rich should make us consider what even our petty Avarice does to us.

In treating ourselves as objects, in the pursuit of mere objects, we are again in the rat race. It distracts us. It makes us distracted on our way to work, at our work, on the way home from work, and even when we are not at work. To be distracted is not just to be out of one's mind, it is not to be in possession of oneself. We have all those other possessions, but we do not possess ourselves. The word comes from the Latin *distractus*, which means "torn apart," and this is the power of Avarice as a sin. It does not leave us whole. We do not engage in the competitiveness of our societies as whole people. "Late and soon, Getting and spending, we lay waste our powers," as Wordsworth says, and our societies incite us day by day to this devastation.

As it is in ourselves, Avarice in our societies is a harassment, difficult to push aside. We are harassed into working in ways that are unsatisfying, so that we may buy things that we have been harassed into believing will satisfy us. What we complain about today in the increased tempo of life is its harassment, and it is caused in part by the Avarice that is naturally in ourselves, but also in the incitement to Avarice that our societies employ at every hour. This is the logic of the economic system that we have created. We know no other way, with the exception of war, or the threat of war, of keeping it going. We tolerate it because we are avaricious for what it spreads before us, temptingly and with cunning; and day by day, we read, mark, learn, and inwardly digest the hymns to it that are chanted by its priests. Hosannah! Hosannah! This is private enterprise! But a society that is so motivated cannot expect to have any moral sanction, or hope to encourage people to be virtuous citizens.

As we know in the case of the miser, Avarice is a form of solitude. We are walled from our neighbors by our possessions, so that they also find us as only one object among all the others. But we then treat our neighbors as mere objects. It has been said by an American sociologist that Americans do not usually make friends or acquaintances but instead make only allies, and it is hard to deny the truth in the observation. When we seek people as allies, we are using them as assets. In other words, we are treating them as objects. Our societies are more and more organized, not merely to encourage this, but to make it all but inevitable and it is yet again the rat race. We now take it almost for granted that we must claw and clamber our way to the top, scaling a pyramid of bodies over which we have trampled, accepting a helping hand from those who are our allies for the time being, but ready at last to let go even of them and climb on their shoulders, as we give ourselves one more push to take the final step ahead of them. It is our Avarice that drives us to be so inhuman.

It is also our Avarice that leaves us no time or energy to care for our neighbors in our society, not just our neighbors but our fellow-citizens as well. We hear of their woes and ills; we would like to do something, but we do not have the time; we are tired at the end of the day; we do not wish to go out again; we have other things on our minds. There is today much talk of the declining participation in the public life and politics of our societies. We say that it is alienation, but that is a fraudulent word, a mere excuse. What we call our alienation is our ennui. To everything about us we respond with Sloth, unless it is to our getting and spending, and part of our Sloth has its sources in our Avarice. When we are as avaricious as we now are—wanting things we do not need—we are really alive to very little else. Avarice is one cause of the dejection that leads to Sloth. We do not know how to think of ourselves except as assets we can use, and so we think of others and the rest of the world. We and they become objects to be manipulated, with no goal but the possessing.

One of the consequences of Avarice that is most strongly condemned in theology is "hardness of heart toward the poor, whether in not giving alms to those in need or harshly exacting payment of debts." In a proclamation that was issued by the Canadian Catholic Conference of Bishops in 1972, it was said: "The riches of Canada are unequally shared. This inequality, which keeps so many people poor, is a social sin." The oppression of the poor is counted as one of the sins that cries out to heaven for vengeance, as also is the defrauding of laborers of their wages. The neglect of our neighbors and the poor is, in the phrase from the Middle Ages, an insensibility to mercy. "Sins against the needy are, in an important sense, the exact opposite of those against the enemy," says William F. May. "The enemy occupies the center of attention. But the needy, at the other extreme, barely exists." These sins of Avarice are sins of omission, and they are nourished in us by our societies. More and more, the poor are tucked away where we cannot see them. More and more, we withdraw from them. We omit to remember them, even in our prayers. Middle-class life in our societies today is increasingly isolated from what is the severest rebuke to it: that it tolerates the persistence of avoidable poverty in societies that it boasts are now marvelously affluent.

St. Paul said that Avarice is the source of all evils, for by riches man acquires the means of committing any sin whatever and of satisfying his desire to sin. We will come to the more precise meaning of this statement, but there is a general sense in which it is true, in which one feels Avarice creeping all over one's nature, amiably tolerated by oneself and by others, and over the whole of our societies. It is so easy to think that one "must have that" and forget the others who need something much more, people to whom one could give in proportion to their needs and one's own resources. No one accuses us of being selfish when we walk into Neiman Marcus and buy a suit or a dress that we do not need, yet a callousness begins to grow in us when our appetites are not challenged. Why should one not dress beautifully? And indeed why should one not? But then something else begins to happen: One gets tired of giving a quarter to a beggar. Or one forgets or simply does not notice.

Much worse than that, one gets tired of supporting, with one's own energy and skills, the programs that might make the beggar not a beggar. The disparity between the "haves" and the "have nots" in our societies, and between the rich and the poor nations, is ceasing to trouble our consciences, and we are far less easily roused to moral indignation at the existence of poverty in our midst than we used to be. We seem to have decided that the poor are always with us, that we may palliate their condition a little, enough at least to prevent any unseemliness of behavior on their part that might embarrass us. Meanwhile we and our societies may just go on getting more and more affluent, and we are satisfied that enough of the wealth will trickle down to those who need it. Our affluent societies have done what could have been predicted; by appealing to our Avarice they have cuts us off from our neighbors who need us.

If we were not so driven and distracted by our covetousness, we might consider that the poor are always with us in a special sense. None of the efforts that we have made to reduce the number of poor and ameliorate their condition seems in the end to have had much effect. Year after year, there they still are. This in turn becomes a convenient rationalization for doing little or nothing about them. Since the programs to assist them did not work in the past, why continue the same or equivalent programs in the future? But what we do not take into account is that, as the condition of the poor is alleviated to some extent, the disparity between them and the well-off remains. They are still poor even if the criteria of poverty have been redefined. The deprival is still as great, even if the conditions have been improved a little, for the deprival of poverty is relative as well as absolute. That we do not recognize this, and do not feel moved to do something about it, is the result of a moral obtuseness in us, which is in turn a result of our Avarice.

Among the evils of Avarice that are condemned by theology is: "Deceit in compassing wealth, commercial dishonesty, overreaching others in trade by unjust methods, and violation of inconvenient contracts." It sounds very like the commercial system under which we live. "It's a time of corruption," said a movie director in Hollywood, when the "irregularities" in the film business came to light. It is characteristic that we should call them "irregularities," which presumably means that they do not happen regularly, even in such a headline as that in the *New York Times*: "Critics of the Movie Business Find Pattern of Financial Irregularities." A pattern of financial irregularities is a system, and we all know that it is a system that is general in our commerce. Yet the words that are used to describe it are mollifying.

The habits that are tolerated by our economic system, indeed on which it is based, in the end spread to the rest of us. If the whole of the commercial system is perceived to be a series of gigantic rip-offs, we can hardly be surprised if the rip-off is accepted as the norm elsewhere in our societies. This is again especially true of the professional middle class, which used to be an exemplar of integrity and also of modesty in the material possessions to which it aspired. Perhaps the lawyer has never been regarded as a model of professional virtue; he has usually been regarded by others as a shyster or worse. But with individual exceptions of course, doctors did not as a class used to be so avaricious. There is now no justification for their fees, except that of an Avarice that has no boundary. The academic and the intellectual are not far behind; the foundations and federal funds are both ready suppliers of their Avarice. The correspondence of writers used to be filled with talk of money because they were poor. Their conversation is now filled with talk of it because they want to be very rich. There is a world of difference. Most clergymen may still be poorly paid, but even they wear the habit of poverty less willingly than before and are not above contrasting their lot with that of others.

There is hardly an institution in our societies now, a body of men and women, leaders of opinion and exemplars of standards, who suggest that poverty may be the proper way of life to choose, not only fitting but rewarding and fulfilling, perhaps the only virtuous way there is. The vow of poverty is not something that we now understand, yet if poverty can be a condition of being a priest, there is no reason why it should not be accepted also by others who administer to us. There is something seriously at fault with a society, something that will in the end destroy us, if poverty that is voluntarily chosen is nowhere celebrated as a good. No other standard is today set against the pursuit of wealth and possessions. From the moment at which the child begins to receive the messages from the society around it, it is subject to the continual pressure of group attitudes that tell it that it will be judged only by success, and that its success will be measured largely by its acquisitiveness. No other model is set before it. The call to a life of poverty in the New Testament is passed over in silence and embarrassment.

This pursuit of wealth and possessions, when conducted with such singlemindedness as it is in our societies, constantly distracts us from spiritual things and not least from the spiritual side of our natures. There is not one person who sets too high a store by wealth and possessions who is not coarsened by them. We use words that make this Avarice seem necessary and even laudable. What can be wrong with *earnings*, with *wages* and *salaries*, with *profits* and *winnings*, with making money legitimately? And of course there is nothing wrong with them, as long as we do not allow them to preoccupy us. This is the sin that the avaricious confess to Dante. "Our eyes would never seek the height, / Being bent on earthly matters," so that "love of all true good was quenched in us / By avarice, and our works were left undone." Their punishment in purgatory is that they must remain prostrate with their eyes bent to the earth. "Heaven has turned our backs to Heaven," they cry. *Adhaesit pavimento anima mea*, they pray, "My soul cleaveth to the dust."

We are in danger in our affluent societies of destroying our humanity as Midas came near to doing. When he was granted one wish by Bacchus whom he had pleased, he asked that everything that he touched might be turned to gold. But finding that this made his food uneatable, he had to ask that the gift be taken away. It is not food that we turn to gold, but much else that we need to nourish our humanity; our punishment may indeed be the opposite of that of Midas, that it is only our wealth that we are at last able to swallow. Crassus "the Rich" was killed in a battle against the Parthians, in which their king Hyrodes, knowing of the notorious avarice of Crassus, ordered that molten gold be poured down his throat. We feel that there is nothing to be said for Midas in myth, or for Crassus in history, that there was a profound inhumanity in their Avarice; yet if only we would look at ourselves, we would find that we are not far from their condition.

The images of Avarice, pagan or Christian, are never attractive. For what we find in Avarice—and why should we think that we may escape it?—is self-love in one of its most perverted forms. Being in love with ourselves, we see other people and things, not as truly themselves and other than us, but as objects that we absorb into our own personalities. We in fact kill the life in everything we touch, just as Midas asked the power to do. It should not be forgotten that we can be avaricious for people, making them reflections of ourselves, wishing to absorb them into our empire, forcing them to acknowledge their dependence, making possessions also of them. As often as not this is done by apparent acts of kindness, by being too solicitous of the well-being of another, as if he or she is incapable of surviving or even of being without one's interest and support. The telephone can be an instrument of this Avarice for others: "I am just calling to see how you are getting on." But they are not calling to see how one is getting on, they are calling to say that one cannot get on without them. They are searching for objects, something else to add to their hoard.

In these last few paragraphs, moving from the deceit of merchants, as the Parson called it, to the deceit of friends, we can see how all-encompassing Avarice is as a sin. This ought not to surprise us. As in all of the sins, the self-love of Pride is never far to trace, drawing everything round itself, and in Avarice this self-love takes a peculiarly odious and perverted form, so that we make objects of all we touch. This is the connection between its material and emotional acquisitiveness. "If you exalt the objects of your love until your picture is a false one; if you idealize them," said Gerald Vann; "if you project upon them your own ideal self, then you are loving not a real person but a dream." The dream of course is of and for oneself, the fantasy of one's own egotism, and this is no less the way in which the avaricious person projects himself on his possessions.

At the heart of Avarice is the evil of waste. Most obviously there is the squandering of the Prodigal Son. We feverishly pursue wealth today, destroying our own lives and those of others in the process, only then to waste it. In saying things like this, one is not being a niggard. There are pleasant things that are naturally desirable, as Aristotle says, and there are others that are not. But there are many that are intermediate between these two, and we are not to be blamed for liking or desiring them, but only for liking them to excess. It is not only our own resources that we waste, when we pursue them beyond a reasonable end, we waste also the resources of our societies and of course of nature. We turn even the bountiful goodness of creation, as it is given to us in nature, into a mere object to serve us, an asset to feed our illusions of self-importance. For there is, as has often been said, something illusory in possessions themselves. What is it that we possess in possessions? "You can't take it with you," as the saying goes, and unless it is something of peculiarly personal value to oneself and to him, what does it really mean to pass it on to an heir? All that one possesses in a possession is security or status or prestige, and although they may in different degrees count for something, the pursuit of them through possessions is usually self-defeating. Those who too obsessively seek security, for example, will usually be more insecure than most.

It is indeed a vain solace that we look for in worldly things. But let us turn the idea of waste on its head. The Parson in his tale points out that Judas complained of waste when Jesus annointed Magdalen. Here is what might at first seem the sharpest contrast with the Prodigal Son, the one intent on squandering his possessions, the other intent on hoarding them. But just as they are the opposite evils of Avarice, prodigality and illiberality, so here they are the reverse sides of the same coin. *Neither of them gives.* The Prodigal Son does not give but wastes. Judas is unwilling to give at all. Aristotle is quite clear that the prodigality is a lesser evil than the illiberality, because the first includes at least some generous impulse and needs only to be brought under control and directed to proper ends, whereas the illiberality is evidence of a stinginess of heart that is hard to correct. The fact remains that in both of them is a lack of giving.

There is no giving if one does not love to whom one gives, and only so does one love what one gives. But how can such love grow if what one has to give is acquired by Avarice? Paul's statement that "The love of money is the root of all evil" is usually taken too lightly. He is warning against the two fundamental evils of Avarice: that the means that one uses to acquire one's possessions are all too likely to be sinful in themselves, and that when the possessions are once acquired they become the means to commit every other sin. Between these two temptations and compulsions there is very little time or room to love what is other than oneself. It has been said by some scholars that the true translation of the text should be: "It is easier for a rope to go through the eye of a needle than for a rich man to enter into the kingdom of God." Whatever its textual accuracy, the image is strong. For in order to go through the eye of the needle, the strands of the rope would have to be frayed away, until there is no more than a thread, and it is this fraying that Avarice causes in us. There is nothing of us left to give, just as we have left nothing of the goods we have to give, and no one whom we have left whole to whom to give. Avarice lays waste our entire world.

Just as he said that an avaricious man would remain avaricious even if he cast his riches into the sea, so Spinoza added that "if a lustful man is downcast, because he cannot follow his bent, he does not, on the grounds of abstention, cease to be lustful." The trap closes tight, in either case, because love has been cast out, and without love no man is free. "Only free men are thoroughly grateful one to another," says Spinoza again, and his words drive home, for what we have been describing all along in Avarice is bondage, in which our humanity is so reduced that we might as well be in the tomb.

Those who have seen the exhibition of Tutankhamen's treasures must in the end find something ghastly in it. We think of the body of the king sealed with his riches for all those centuries in a dark and airless chamber. When it is opened, his body has decomposed, but the gold and the alabaster have kept their substance and form, and glitter as brightly as ever. What is absent from them is the king himself. They tell us of his majesty—in other words, of his status—but they tell us nothing of the man. They are relics of a civilization in which, under the sway of its cosmology and beliefs, the king was as depersonalized and dehumanized as his subjects. We look back at the treasures; with all their brilliance and art they are decadent and meaningless. We think again of the king among his treasures—an object only, buried among other objects. It was they that survived. Perhaps we have gone to the exhibition in such large numbers because we are looking at something we can understand: at the contents of a tomb from which, when the stone was rolled away, it was the objects and not the man that rose again, in which the man had become the most lifeless of all the objects. If we look straightforwardly at our societies now, how can we deny that this is an image of us?

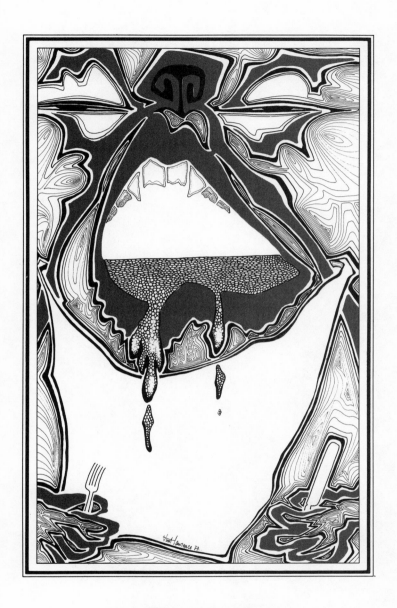

CHAPTER SIX
GLUTTONY or GULA

GLUTTONY OR GULA

WATCH A GLUTTONOUS man at his food. His napkin is tucked in his collar and spread across his paunch, announcing the seriousness of the business in which he is engaged. His bulging face and popping eyes are fixed on his plate. Only occasionally does he look up at his companions with a glazed look. His mouth has only one function, as an orifice into which to push his food. Now and then he may grunt at what someone has said. Otherwise he stuffs. He is like a hog at its swill. He may ignore his companions; but they cannot ignore him. Even if they can avert their eyes from the spectacle—the swamp in his mouth, where the tide ebbs and flows, the seepage from its corners—they are unable to block their ears to the noise. He sucks each spoonful through his teeth as if it were the Sargasso Sea. He does not chew his meat but champs and chomps, crunches and craunches. He crams, gorges, wolfs, and bolts. He might as well be alone. As with all the sins, Gluttony makes us solitary. We place ourselves apart, even at a table of sharing.

This solitude to which the sins condemn us is partly a result of taking something in our lives, which has its appropriate place and value, and then lifting it out of place and exaggerating its importance to us. In the end, it is no longer a part of our lives but takes the place of living. Avarice does this with possessions, Lust with sex, and Gluttony does it with food. But in the process a distortion takes place. Avarice is more interested in possessing than in the possession, Lust in sexual activity than in sexual feeling, and Gluttony is more interested in eating than in the food. It is the appetites in themselves, and their need for gratification, that take over one's life, and the object of each appetite, which might in itself be pleasing, is submerged in the inordinate desire for it. The food on the plate of the glutton is not really the source of pleasure to him.

John Masefield placed the glutton with the idler and the fool and said that the characteristic of all three is a "carelessness of life and beauty." Gluttony does not find any beauty in food. Its taste and color do not interest him. He does not care how it is arranged and not very much how it is cooked. Food can and sometimes ought to be an enchantment. It can please our eyes, before it pleases our taste, and it may please us even in memory. For none of this does the glutton care. If a dish that is as beautifully arranged as it has been excellently cooked is brought to the table—perhaps with its sauce browned so delicately, as Virginia Woolf once described a succulent meal, that it is flecked like the side of a doe—the glutton does not exclaim that it almost seems a pity to spoil it. He wants only to get his hands on it; if he could have his own way, probably to get them into it. The ridge of grapes down the back of a sole veronique under their coverlet of dappled sauce mean as little to him as the subtle flavor of the shallots and the white wine in which the fish was cooked and from which the sauce has been made. He might as well eat at a trough.

There is a sinfulness in allowing an appetite to make one so indifferent to beauty, to give no thought to delicacy and graciousness; and even away from the table, the glutton is still a boor, as unappreciative of a painting or a piece of music, a poem or simply a jewel, as he is of his food. He would grunt if shown a Grecian urn. He has no sense of what is only itself and so is irreplaceable. Not even his food is precious to him. When we say that the glutton makes a pig of himself, we do not mean only that he has his trotters in his slop, but that the rarest delicacy can be set before him, and it will still be to him only slop. Gluttony does not give a particular value to anything it consumes. It does not savor. It only devours. Although the glutton eats voraciously, he does not even eat with gusto. One would never say of him that he has a healthy appetite.

Just as each of the sins is leashed with others, so our knowledge of one informs our knowledge of the rest. There is a disregard of beauty in all of the sins. This may be only another way of saying that they are all loveless. Not seeing what is the Other, with open eyes and open heart, they do not see what is beautiful in it. More of us are blinder than we think. But it is worth sticking for the moment to the precise point. The sins do not let us see and appreciate what is beautiful. Pride is offended by beauty in anything but itself. Envy cannot bear the sight of it. Anger will destroy it if it cannot possess it. Sloth simply does not have the spirit or the energy to enjoy beauty. Avarice sees in the Other's beauty only its own reflection. Lust thinks that it seeks and finds beauty but never knows how to be pleased by it. Gluttony also has this failing, and the ugliness of our picture of the glutton is only a mirror of the ugliness to which he reduces all that he touches. A glutton does not even know how to lick an ice cream cone and leave it to the very end still an ice cream cone.

If food and drink can and sometimes should be an enchantment, they are also necessary to our existence. Gluttony and Lust are the only sins that abuse something that is essential to our survival. It seems right that they stand together. A disrespect for food is a disrespect for creation, for the goodness and bounty of it, for what has been provided to sustain us as a part of it—not only as a part of it, but as the only species with some degree of mastery over it, and so with a special responsibility to it. None of this crosses the mind of the glutton. He does not respect his food; he is not even grateful for it. One cannot imagine him saying grace before a meal, which is a prayer of thankfulness for life and not merely for the food we are about to eat. Gluttony is particularly a sin against the rest of created things, against what we now rather feebly call our environment.

But few of us today say grace. We take for granted, not merely a sufficiency of food, but a plenitude of it: what not so long ago, in the lifetime of many, was counted as a blessing. A grace was not only a prayer of thankfulness. It bestowed on our foods our sense that these also are a part of creation, that they are God's things that we eat, out of his boundless goodness to us, and therefore with all the more reason to be thankful and for us to honor them. One might smile at the English headmaster who, while the Battle of the Atlantic was raging, pronounced the benediction before lunch: "For what we are about to receive, thank God and the British Merchant Navy." But the incongruity made its point. That their food was precious, that it came to them, not as a right, but as a privilege, this every schoolboy could understand, even though the rations were scant and unappetizing, and the headmaster was certainly eating better behind their backs.

The amount and variety of foods that we now expect to find, at all times of day and night, in our supermarkets and gourmet shops, restaurants and cafeterias, and even in our health food stores, is what would in the Old Testament have been called an abomination unto the Lord. In saying so, one is not being an ascetic, and certainly not highmindedly recommending asceticism to others, especially when it is not one's own bent. There is nothing depraved in itself in having such an amount and variety of food available to a large number of people, and we cannot now make it unavailable, unless we choose to manage our societies like East Berlin. If fruits and vegetables can be flown from coast to coast, even continent to continent, all the year round, at prices that enough people can afford, they will be flown from coast to coast, continent to continent, all the year round. Life ought not to be kept drab and gray, if it can be made varied and colorful. But we need to be on guard. We enjoy not just an abundance of foods in our affluent societies, but a superabundance of them, what Shakespeare in *Coriolanus* called "enough, with over-measure." Waste is a sin and, in some ways, is a branch of all the sins. There is in Gluttony a waste, not only of what we consume, but of our energy in consuming it.

The problem with this overmeasure, as with all excess, is that it may enslave us, that it is almost certain to do so. Here we now are, released from the preoccupation of wondering whether we will eat tomorrow, from the monotony of diets that will not vary much from day to day for most of our lives, released even from the bondage of the peasant woman to her stock pot, and what do we do? We return to the slavery of the kitchen, but now to make a fetish of it. We have become absurdly interested in our food. We think, read, worry, talk about it. We expect it to be too foolproof a nourishment—of our spirits as well as our bodies—to enchant us too continuously. Our attitude to it is also idolatrous. We have made of our food a golden calf. "We are what we eat," we used to say glibly, but now we seem to believe it. Food is the miracle drug by which we set most store. There is more addiction to the icebox than to the medicine chest.

This idolatry has its scripture. Forests must die to provide paper for the cookery books that spill endlessly from the publishing houses each year. The 1974-75 Supplement to *Books in Print* had 193 entries under Cookery; in the 1975-76 volume there were 208; and 197 followed the next year. Even allowing for the repetition of a few titles, the figures are hard to believe, for these are new books that were published or announced in the years in question. Satiated by *The Eating Rich Cookbook* we may turn to *Staples, Delicacies & Curiosities from the Earth's Humble Kitchens*. There is *The Presbyterian Ladies Cookbook* and the loftier *We Gather Together: A Cook Book of Menus & Dishes by the Wives of Bishops of the Episcopal Church*, and in the same religious vein, there is also the unabashed *Cooking with God*, a collection of recipes from the Near East. When we have had our fill of *Love at First Bite*—there is clearly some strain on authors and publishers to find titles for so many works in the same limited field—we can move on to *The Art of Cooking with Love and Wheatgerm*. And of course there are the guides to eating places. Those who have exhausted *The Underground Gourmet* can graduate to *The San Francisco Underground Gourmet*. Whether or not our tables groan with food, our kitchen shelves groan with books about it. They are often now the only library in a house.

In the past decade and a half, Craig Claiborne has presented us with his old testament, his new testament, his apocrypha, and his exegeses and commentaries on his original texts. From *The New York Times Cook Book* in 1961, to *The New York Times Menu Cook Book* in 1966, to *Craig Claiborne's Kitchen Primer* in 1969, to *Cooking with Herbs & Spices* in 1970, to *Classical French Cooking* in the same year, to *The New York Times International Cook Book* in 1971, to *The Chinese Cookbook* in 1972, and at last to *Craig Claiborne's Favorites from the New York Times* in 1975, which he topped with *Craig Claiborne's Notebooks from the New York Times* a year later. Must one not marvel at the industry and the ingenuity? We cannot be too solemn about it. But when we think of the generations that were content with a single book from Mrs. Beeton, our interest today in what we put in our stomachs seems excessive, even to the point of lunacy.

An invitation to dinner has, in many cases, become a hazard. What used to be a sociable occasion has been turned into a form of solitude. The hostess or host—for when they take up cooking as a fine art, men are the worst offenders—will hardly be with their guests. They will be in the kitchen. But that is not all. The guests in turn are hardly permitted to be with each other. As each course is brought to the table, it must be tasted, discussed, each ingredient told, the method of preparation recounted at length, praised, vaunted: literally *ad nauseam,* which is not the effect that good eating is meant to produce, except in some distant cultures. All other conversation is merely an entracte as the real drama unfolds with each dish. This is no less a form of solitude than that of the glutton at his trough. All companionship is destroyed. The guests might as well have stayed at home and read *The Art of French Cooking,* or watched Julia Child whip up a soufflé on television. At least they would not have had to applaud her.

In the department stores, the cooking ware used to be in the basement, a few necessary items of kitchen equipment, but now it spills over one of the main floors, taking up more and more room each year, ever more elaborately designed and ever more expensive. It is now almost impossible to buy a rolling pin that is just a rolling pin; and if one is lucky enough to find one, it will be in an antique shop for thirty-five dollars as an *objet d'art* for one's mantelpiece or bookshelves. (The books are in the kitchen, the kitchen equipment is on the bookshelves.) There is nothing wrong with the designing of functional things so that they will also be beautiful, but there is something very wrong in the exaltation of merely useful things to objects of false veneration. The kind of cooking ware that is now available in such profusion is again an expression of idolatry: These are the beautiful things with which we will reverence the golden calf of our food. For it is not the food itself, a fit and estimable thing in its place, that interests those who exalt it. They turn it into something that it is not and replace other worthwhile things with it.

It may be agreed that our obsession with eating is one of the most widespread expressions of idolatry in our age, but we usually think of gluttony as so unsightly and bloated that few of us today may seem guilty of it. On the one hand, there are the dieters and calorie counters; on the other, the addicts of health foods. No one now seems able to rise in the morning and go out to meet the world without stepping on the bathroom scales. These may seem to reflect a self-denying abstemiousness, but there is Gluttony in all of them. (Fastidiousness in eating is regarded in theology as just as much a fault of the sin as excess in it.) Each of them shows an inordinate interest in eating, even though it may appear to be in not eating. They make their own fetish of eating, no less than the glutton with whom we are more familiar. They are just as obsessed with their food, even if their attention is fixed only on a raw carrot and a prune; and their refrigerators and their larders tell, not merely of the time, but of the energy and the anxiety that they give to the most natural of functions.

It is worth watching the obsessive dieters. They are constantly going to their refrigerators, perhaps more than anyone else, even when it is not yet time for their rations, counting what is there, making sure that not one item is missing of what has become so precious to them. They gaze on the morsels, fondle them, even rearrange them, each in its sack, all lovingly known and enumerated. From hour to hour they return to make an inventory. When *in extremis,* they count the spinach leaves. But at last the bell rings. It is mealtime. Salivating like Pavlov's dogs, they scurry to the kitchen table with a stick of celery, a radish, a spoonful of cottage cheese, and a dried apricot for dessert. Watch them as they eat. They devour their delicacies just as the conventional glutton sucks up his bouillabaisse. Their eyes also are fixed on their plates.

They occupy the rest of their days by reading and

thinking about food. There must be some new regimen that they should be following, one more impurity that has been discovered in the endive. Whether they are eating or not, their minds are on their food and what their food is doing to their bodies. (Their obsession with it is destroying their minds, but that does not bother them.) What is there to say about six segments of orange on a bed of dandelion leaves, one may ask, but one should not underestimate the inventiveness of an absorbing interest. From so unpromising a beginning, an entire discourse will be developed on the relative dangers and benefits of cyanocobalamin, thiamine, pantothenic acid, riboflavin, glucose, dextrose, dextro-glucose, sucrose, galactose, melibiose, hemoglobin, lecithoprotein, cytoglobin, and (for it must not be forgotten) phosphoaminolipide. There is neither time nor need to talk of anything else. The interest is gluttonous and, as with all forms of Gluttony, the end is solitude. For none of the activity needs a companion. The driving motive of the dieter is again an inordinate self-love.

This is no less true of the addicts of health foods, as they exclaim at the wholesomeness of a sassafras nut or hymn ecstatically the savor of a sunflower seed. They also may not seem to be gluttons in the common sense, yet their interest in their eating is again a form of Gluttony. It is disproportionate and unnatural. There is a great deal of the fastidiousness of self-love in it. A creaturely thing is magnified beyond its actual significance and made some kind of expression of oneself. One of the pleasures of food, as even theology admits, is that it offers occasions for social intercourse. But it is precisely this that is refused by the dieters and addicts of health foods. Eating is their one staple of interest and conversation. By giving to food a false value, they also rob it of its real value. In contrast to them and to the more familiar glutton, the gourmet thinks and talks very little about his food, except at the moment of preparation or appreciation. At the gourmet's table one notices the food, expresses a brief appreciation of the savor, and expands about other things.

This obsession with one's food is a reflection of an obsession with our bodies. It is another kind of whiffling activity, a way of filling in the time for people who now have more leisure than they know how to use, an artificial interest for those with too few real interests. Conversation about dieting has merely taken the place of coffee klatches, which anyhow can no longer be held unless the coffee is caffeine-free. One knows from one's own experience that those who take too fastidious an interest in themselves seldom have the time or the inclination to take much interest in anyone else. They are consumed with self-love. When their eyes are not on the bathroom scales, they are on the mirror. They seem to carry invisible mirrors with them, and constantly to be consulting them even as they look straight at oneself. The old adage, "A little of what you fancy does you good," meant that one ate without fuss, and had done with it. Eating was put in its place. One inhabits one's body, without its being a prison, and turns to the world.

We can be gluttons for punishment, as we say, and we can be gluttons for work. We can also be gluttons for youthfulness, and at the root of the excessive interest in dieting there is a fear of aging. There is in fact a fear of dying. We can be gluttons for life. We should of course love life, but it also must be given its appropriate value. We must be prepared to sacrifice it for some purposes, which does not mean only in a heroic deed, but by asking our bodies sometimes to accept an unusual strain, for which they will have to pay a price. The people whose faces are unlined after a certain age are people whom we distrust. They have done nothing that cost them anything, suffered nothing, and we suspect that in the end they are nothing. The beauty that they have so carefully preserved would crumble at a touch. It has not been made with others or for others. The facelift is a mask, perhaps the most grotesque of all; age is to be denied, even while the grave waits.

Our age is gluttonous for drugs. "To use narcotics in small doses and only occasionally is a venial sin if done without sufficient reason. . . . To use drugs in greater quantities so as to lose the use of one's reason is in itself a mortal sin; but for a good reason [as in the case of an operation] it is permissible." This is the discriminating language of theology. It is as a form of Gluttony that drug-taking is condemned, and our tolerance of it is a part of our tolerance of Gluttony. Our affluent societies make them more available to us than ever before, and we snatch them up like the foods at the supermarket. Taking drugs in excess is regarded as a grievous sin, because they may cause serious harm to one's health and because they are likely to deprive one of the use of one's reason. When every experiment has been tried, and every apologia has been offered, there is no way of denying that drugs, as they are today used in our societies, are damaging on both counts; only a society that has grown listless about its members, about its own future, and about the continuance of the human endeavor, could be so idly acquiescent in their widespread and malignant use.

The young drug-takers in the 1960s had a point when they said that they had taken their first lessons from their parents' medicine cabinets. Pill-popping today is a part of the middle-class way of life, and before those who indulge in it proceed to a daily series of "uppers" and "downers," they have already acquired the habit from the indiscriminate prescription of drugs, often for the most minor and even imaginary of ailments. There is a level of pain that we ought to be able and willing to endure, if the only alleviation is the too-ready use of drugs, which either reduce our vitality or artificially stimulate in ways that also lead to physical and nervous prostration. We may learn from people who are suffering from terminal cancer. They often decide that some of the pain is worth enduring, rather than surrender what preciously remains of their lives to so comatose and insensible a state that even they do not know themselves any longer and in fact might just as well not be living. In contrast to them, there are normally healthy people who deaden themselves with mere aspirin, rather than let a headache take its course, and whom one suspects of sometimes inducing headaches in themselves as an excuse for taking yet more aspirin. This is Gluttony, and it is wholly reasonable that, among the foods at our supermarkets, there should be an array of nonprescription drugs, merely for the picking. We write our own Rx for the drugs we want and pay for them with the Rice Krispies.

Of all the gluttons, perhaps the most evident is, and always has been, the habitual drunkard. Paul says in his epistle to the Galatians that drunkenness is numbered among the sins that exclude from heaven, a warning that one is unfortunately apt to overlook at the very moment when it is most needed. The drunkard is condemned because he also "deprives himself of the use of reason," and because he "makes himself resemble the irrational brute beast, destroying in himself the likeness to God." For the sin to be grievous the drunkenness must be habitual, and the loss of reason "should be total and continuous for some time." These discriminations draw attention, not only to the destruction of a whole human nature that takes place, but to the fact that the sin of Gluttony is willed, as are all the sins, that when we talk of habitual drunkenness we are not talking of inadvertence, of something we cannot help doing.

We ought not to speak too easily of drunkenness, or of any of the other forms of Gluttony, as only or always a sickness. There may be physical and even psychological conditions that make some people more liable than others to take drink or drugs too heavily, or be more susceptible to them, but by far the greater part of Gluttony among us is willful. The word "alcoholic" should be reserved for those who, like the kleptomaniac, are powerless to refrain from what they are doing. By this test we are not justified in regarding even all habitual drunkards as alcoholics. The majority of gluttons, including the habitual drug-takers and drunkards, meet the definition of sinning: that "there must be both advertence to the evil and free consent to it." We today have too many psychological explanations that destroy the very idea of our will, and it is one of the values of the idea of sin that it emphasizes, in the words of Henry Cardinal Manning, that there is "the knowledge of the intellect of what we are doing, [and] the consent of the will in doing it."

"Gluttony tends to be, on the whole, a warm-hearted and companionable sin," says Dorothy Sayers, "often resulting from, and in, a mistaken notion of good-fellowship." One of course knows what she means and does not wish to come down with a heavy hand on any enjoyment. But it must be remembered that she herself says that the notion from which Gluttony springs is mistaken, and in talking of the sin we are (as with all of them) talking of excess. As we have seen, Gluttony may make use of the occasions of companionship, but it destroys them. The gluttonous man at his swill, the dieters who are fretful about their eating, the person who is stoned, the drunkard who disappears in the bottle—they are all people who remove themselves from any caring for others, even from their companions at the moment, and who in fact remove themselves from the concern that others feel for them. It is because it so misuses what ought to be enchantments that Gluttony seems so perverted and disgusting a form of self-love.

We have said that it is particularly the sin against the rest of created things. It is out of Gluttony, which is intent on consuming, more than out of Avarice, which is mainly interested in possessing, that we eat up the raw materials and natural resources of the earth. The glutton's contempt for the bounty of creation is reflected in each of us and in our societies, in the insatiable appetite with which we burn up "all things bright and beautiful" that have been provided for our well-being. "Only in so far as a man remains fully sensitive, open, receptive, and, indeed, vulnerable to his environment," says William F. May, "does he reckon with it in its full diversity and splendor." It is true that we now seem to be alert to the consequences of our evil-doing in this respect, but it is only when some particularly vile desecration of created things can no longer be ignored, or when we are abruptly confronted with the imminent shortage of some raw material on which we have relied, in other words when our own standard of living is threatened. Our essential depravity remains. Encouraged and provoked by our societies, we still wish to consume as if they are necessities, not only more and more luxuries, but more and more elaborate ones, each of which can in the end be enjoyed only by recklessly depleting the natural resources of our world.

What is more, we consume most, perhaps, simply by our wastefulness. If waste is at the heart of Sloth, it is at the heart also of Gluttony. We discard clothing before it is worn out. Our drawers are full of sweaters and shirts, our closets of suits and dresses, worn for a season, if at all, and then as forgotten as if they had never been bought. Of all the food that is set before us, in stores and restaurants, and which we buy for our own use at home, an unthinkable amount goes into the trash can or down the garbage disposal. The packaging is itself a form of waste. Butter comes to us in restaurants and cafeterias with a piece of cardboard beneath the slice and a piece of paper on top of it. Both the cardboard and the paper are made from something that has its own value. Sugar is not served to us in bowls but in paper satchels. Cream does not come in jugs but in plastic tubs. Jelly is not in a bowl but in a plastic container. After a family of four has breakfast at a restaurant, the table is a litter of empty and half-empty containers of paper and plastic that, multiplied several million times a day, amount to a vicious waste of the resources from which they are manufactured.

The packaging in turn makes it more and more difficult to buy the exact amount or quantity of whatever we want. If we need seven one-inch nails, we have to purchase a packet of three dozen, two dozen of which are of lengths for which we have no use, and five of the one-inch nails we do not need. Strawberries are in baskets wrapped in cellophane, so that we cannot weigh the exact amount that we want. We may want three handkerchiefs; we have to buy a packet of six. Even the child cannot go in with its nickel and buy a nickel's worth of candy. It must buy as much as the manufacturer has decided is convenient and profitable to package and sell. There was far less waste in the old grocery, hardware store, haberdashery, and of course the general store. But our wastefulness has become a way of life. If our Avarice makes us buy what we do not need, we are forced by our own Gluttony and by our gluttonous societies to buy more than we want, even of what we do need, and a whole psychology of plenty settles without any challenge into our deepest being.

We begin not to think what we mean by a high standard of living. There is nothing in itself wrong with a high standard of living. The most urgent task that faces us is to ensure that more people throughout the world and in our own societies are able to enjoy one. But it becomes too easy to confuse a high standard of living with a mere greed for the good things of life, and above all an excessive indulgence in bodily comforts. We cannot but be damaged by our tolerance of this greed. Unconsciously, we begin to put first what ought to be last. *Labia mea Domine.* . . is the prayer of the gluttonous in purgatory: "O Lord, open thou my lips, and my mouth shall show forth Thy praise." The appropriateness of the prayer is that it reminds them that the mouth was made for other things than eating and drinking. When we let Gluttony grow in us, it is these other things that we forget. Dante makes a telling leap from our everyday Gluttony to Adam's and Eve's eating of the apple.

For there is something else in it all. There is in the sin of Gluttony, not least in its wastefulness, the sin of ingratitude. The praise that we should show forth to God should in part be a praise of thankfulness. But, as we have said, the glutton does not say grace, and neither do many of us. Nor does the glutton show much thanks at the table of his host or hostess. Ingratitude is one of the most mean-minded consequences of self-love. It makes life charmless. It withholds recognition from others and what they do usually selflessly to please. If one stops to think for a moment, one realizes that there is ingratitude in all the sins. Pride cannot see anything for which it ought to be grateful. Envy is unable to be grateful for what it has. Anger never stops to think that perhaps it has reason for gratitude rather than for ire. Avarice is never grateful for having just what it needs. Sloth has not the energy to be grateful. Lust feels no gratitude to those with whom it lies. But it is in Gluttony that we can most clearly find this meanness of spirit, and feel most immediately the cutting off of all community, simply by the inability to be thankful to others.

It is too easy to dismiss Gluttony in all its forms as no more than a relatively harmless overindulgence in whatever we crave. Its origins and its effects are far more serious than that, otherwise it would not be included among the deadly sins. When we think in the end of the glutton, one of our strongest impressions is of his tedium. He does not just lapse into torpor at the moment of his gross satiation; his life is itself one of torpor from which his indulgence is an escape. The atmosphere at a Roman banquet was one of boredom and the attempt to escape from it, of a lassitude that nevertheless had something desperate about it, and the same is hardly less true of those whom we may see today dining extravagantly night after night. All has palled; all is jaded. But if we think that this tedium touches only the wealthy, we are guilty of the sin of thinking that we do not sin. There is a general tedium in the profusion of our affluent societies. We may not all have our faces buried in our swill to escape it, but we all have them buried in some overrichness of indulgence, some activity that will merely take our minds off our emptiness.

The Gluttony of our own age—including the drug-takers with their "uppers" and "downers," and the inordinate interest of the dieters in what they eat—has at least a part of its cause, perhaps even the main part, in the boredom of our societies. When there is so much to do, when so much is spread before us for our titillation, surely we should not be bored. Yet it is all so dissatisfying, with neither purpose nor deep reward. Gluttony is a grievous sin, according to theology, if it induces us to find all our contentment in the gratifying of our appetites. But this is today almost all that our societies offer us, the only strenuousness of activity to which we are excited. We are left with a hollow at our core, a sinking feeling in our spirits from day to day, and we resort to the device of the glutton in his private life, one which is well known to the psychiatrist in the patient who overeats as a compensation for some emotional lack. We will fill and stuff our emptiness, even if it is only by chewing ravenously on a raw carrot. We are becoming a breed of junkies. If our societies are founded on Avarice, the state to which they reduce us is Gluttony. With the sin already in us, we do not stir ourselves to resist.

CHAPTER SEVEN
LUST or LUXURIA

LUST or LUXURIA

LUST IS NOT interested in its partners, but only in the gratification of its own craving, not in the satisfaction of our whole natures, but only in the appeasement of an appetite that we are unable to subdue. It is therefore a form of self-subjection, in fact, of self-emptying. The sign it wears is: "This property is vacant." Anyone may take possession of it for a while. Lustful people may think that they can choose a partner at will for sexual gratification. But they do not really choose. They accept what is available. Lust accepts any partner for a momentary service; anyone may squat in its groin. It has nothing to give, and so it has nothing to ask.

Love has meaning only insofar as it includes the idea of its continuance. Even what we rather glibly call a love affair, if it comes to an end, may continue as a memory that is pleasing in our lives; we can renew the sense of privilege and reward of having been allowed to know someone with such intimacy and sharing. But Lust dies at the next dawn, and when it returns in the evening, to search where it may, it is with its own past erased. Love wants to enjoy in other ways the human being whom it has enjoyed in bed; it looks forward to having breakfast. But in the morning Lust is always furtive. It dresses as mechanically as it undressed and heads straight for the door, to return to its own solitude. Like all the sins, it also makes us solitary. It is self-abdication at the very core of one's own being, a surrender of our need and ability to give and receive. Lust does not come with open hands, certainly not with an open heart. It comes only with open legs. Perhaps above everything—for it seems to summarize it all—Lust is charmless. It is charmless with what should have most charm.

Love is involvement as well as continuance, but Lust will not get involved. This is one of the forms in which we may see it today. If people now engage in indiscriminate and short-lived relationships more than in the past, it is not really for some exquisite sexual pleasure that is thus gained but because they refuse to become involved and to meet the demands that love will make. They are asking for little more than servicing, such as they might get at a gas station. The fact that one may go to bed with a lot of people is, in itself, less Lust's offense than the fact that one goes to bed with people for whom one does not care, for whom there is never any intention that one will care.

The characteristic of the "singles" today is not the sexual freedom that they are supposed to enjoy, but the fact that this freedom is a deception. They are free with only a fraction of their natures. The full array of human emotions is hardly involved. The "singles bar" does not have an obnoxious odor because its clients, before the night is over, may hop into bed with someone whom they have just met, but because they do not consider that, beyond the morning, either of them may care for the other. As they have made deserts of themselves, so they make deserts of their beds. This is the sin of Lust. Just as it dries up human beings, so it dries up human relationships. The atmosphere in a singles bar is of dried-up, stale, uninterested, lethargic, mechanical, unfeeling, uninvolved, unrewarding, tedious, boring, let's-get-it-over-with, tomorrowless, dull, empty, self-emptying sex.

The word that comes to mind, when one thinks of Lust, is "parched." Everyone in a singles bar seems to have lost moisture. The one odor that is absent from it, in fact, is the odor of sex, just as it is absent from a strip-tease. "Exotic nudes!" says the sign outside the shabby bar. If only they were! This is peculiarly the achievement of Lust: to make the flesh seem parched, to deprive it of all real voluptuousness of feeling. Puritans too often worry about the wrong things. The offense of our age is not that it excites sex, but that it withers it, takes away all dewiness from it, shrivels it to a husk. The reason why Lust often turns to perversions is that the flesh itself has ceased to please it.

Lust is not a sin *of* the flesh so much as a sin *against* it. It is in our flesh that we are present to the rest of creation, and particularly we are present in it to each other, revealing and exposing, sensitive to others and even vulnerable to them, open to hurt. When one hears people talk today of the sexual act as if it were rather like emptying one's bladder, one wishes to remind them that people still get hurt. They get hurt in their bodies, not merely from slappings and beatings, but from more subtle humiliations of which our sexual feelings are registers. Lust is a humiliation of the flesh, of another's and of one's own; and it is a perversity of our times that, in the name of a freedom that is delusive, we not only tolerate this humiliation, but exalt it as a wonder of the modern age, like the lighthouse at Pharos.

A student who submitted himself to the inquiries of Alfred Kinsey said afterward that, no matter what answers he gave to the questions, Kinsey just kept on asking him, "But how many times?" Much in the same way, we have reduced love to sex, sex to the act, and the act to a merely quantitative measurement of it. Sexual love can have infinite expressions, not all of which need to be consummated in the act, and it is this variety of expression that Lust must always diminish. It is not only solitary but uninventive in the slaking of its thirst. Whatever may be said for the sexual investigations that we now pursue and read so avidly, it cannot be denied that they are rather one-dimensional in their approach to the questions they raise. "People now seem to have sex on their minds," Malcolm Muggeridge once said, "which is a peculiar place to have it." Our obsession with sex is in a fact a misplacing and trivialization of it. Our preoccupation is such that it has no association with the rest of our lives.

More than we care to admit, we have all become voyeurs. "We live in an age in which voyeurism is no longer the side line of the solitary deviate," writes William F. May, "but rather a national pastime, fully institutionalized and naturalized in the mass media." Once again the puritan makes the mistake of thinking that to have sex continually on view is an incitement to it. It in fact weakens the feelings and passions that sex can and should arouse. Pornographic literature and movies do not incite us to strenuous emulation. On the contrary, they are substitutes, evidence not of the strength of our sexual feelings, but of their enfeeblement. We can and usually do indulge in pornography by ourselves; no one else has to be there, and we have to do nothing with even our own sexuality, except possibly to manipulate ourselves. It is a substitute again for involvement with another person. If it makes us lust at all, it is not for sexual experience with someone else, but merely for the empty cravings and gratifications of Lust itself. We reduce ourselves to the final absurdity: that we will lust after Lust.

Pornography is another way of condemning ourselves to solitariness. It is as such that it is a form of Lust, and as such that it may be regarded as sinful. But like other forms of Lust, it is sinful also because it is an atrophying. (Theology condemns what it calls sexual anesthesia.) In other words, it is a form of dying. What is left to Lust when its cravings at last subside, as subside in the end they will? It is alone. It has died. It has made no bonds and is in the desert that it has made, with no longer even a craving. It is in its own black hole, where no voice can reach it, and from which its own voice cannot be heard. It has collapsed into nothingness. It has burned itself out. Our excessive fear of old age is the fear that must be expected in a society in which Lust has been made a dominating motive. We would not fear it so much if we did not fear that it would be empty; and we would not fear so much that it will be empty if we had not emptied our lives already in the pursuit of mere cravings.

It is significant that we say we lust after a person or object. Lust is always in pursuit and ends as empty-handed as it began. This is why we have to condemn the character of Don Juan, even if, again, not for the reasons of the puritans. To be interested only in pursuit and not in the attainment, to give so much of one's energy to the practice only of seduction, is a prescription for making a desert of one's world and oneself. "Promiscuous love necessitates hypocrisy," Christopher Sykes has said. "To play the part of Don Juan, you have to be word-perfect in that of Tartuffe as well." Such hypocrisy is again a form of self-emptying. We become only the words and roles in which we are so versed, and at last we cannot find who we are behind them. We become only our fronts, hardly more than cardboard figures. The play of seduction, if it is to be rewarding to the seducer as well as the seduced, requires that the whole personalities of each be engaged. If love is a journey into another land, as Rebecca West once called it, then seduction ought to be part of a mutual exploration, to see if the land may be entered and enjoyed together. Lust is incapable of this play, it is not interested in exploring, it does not want to enter any land. Perhaps most terrible, it has no personality of its own to bring to the encounter, with which it may bring into play the personality of the other and respond fully itself.

If love is continuance and involvement, perhaps it is no less attention, a constancy of gaze on the object of one's love, so that one grows to know it, as other than oneself, in all the richness and variety of its own character. Lust is incapable of this constancy; it has no attention to give. The time-span of its interest is determined by the clockwork to which it has reduced its desires. We seem to be embarrassed to talk today of fidelity, to give it much of a precedence, even though we may observe all around us that people still get hurt by unfaithfulness. If we will not speak of fidelity, then perhaps we can talk of constancy. The trouble with sexual infidelity is that it directs the constancy of our attention to someone else. We remove a part of our gaze, and turn it elsewhere. In fact we remove a part of ourselves and give it elsewhere. What comes between a couple when one of them is unfaithful is, not the other woman or the other man, but what now cannot be shared by them.

This is why any sensitive person is intuitively aware when the other is being unfaithful. He or she knows almost at once that something has been withdrawn, that there is something that the other is unable to bring and share. If a mere sexual act were all that is involved, unfaithfulness would not be such an everlasting problem. But even if it is possible to "have sex" (the phrase is revealing) with someone else without loving that person, the fact that no love has been bestowed elsewhere does not mean that none has been withdrawn. It is rarely that unfaithfulness does its damage in a single affair. Its danger is that it erodes. Piecemeal it chips away at a relationship, not only at the constancy of our love, but at last at our capacity to love. If not in the beginning, in the end it is a form of Lust: not so much for the obvious reason that we wish to engage in sexual relations with other people, but because it finally is another way of emptying ourselves of our ability to express and use our whole natures in a relationship that commands our allegiance.

It empties us of our capacity for loyalty, until we

become incapable of forming an enduring relationship with any one individual. Our relationships are frayed from the start, like cut-off jeans, because we are no longer able to discover the unconditional worth of another human being, or ultimately of oneself. Love requires some effort, but our age encourages us to avoid it, by refusing to get involved and when involved to escape from it. At the first itch of dissatisfaction, the first rankle of difficulty, we can sever the knot, with as little ado as possible, and go to the other side of the fence where we know that it will be greener. This weakness of our allegiance does not affect only our personal relationships. It begins to run through all that we do. We find that we become incapable of giving loyalty to anything. If we do not set much store by being loyal to those who are closest to us, how will we be loyal to the neighbors in our societies for whom we are also responsible? When people say today that they are not their brother's keeper, it is not all callousness as such that they are revealing, so much as a diminishing of their capacity for loyalty, the refusal to be committed to and responsible for others. They keep themselves free to go from whim to whim, answerable to nobody and nothing but themselves.

The question of attention is important. We cannot hope to love a picture, or a piece of music, or a poem, without giving it our attention. We need to "gaze" on it, not once but again; to return to it, in different moods, for different reasons; to let it speak to us, to learn how to hear it; to notice that it has many aspects, that it is never quite the same, that it has new things to tell. Only in this way do we get to know it and so to love it for what it is, not to impose ourselves on it, taking from it only what we want. This attention needs no less to be given to someone we love. The gaze does not peer, it learns how to look and, learning how to look, learns how to love. Knowing the object well, it leaves it still itself. This kind of attention, above all the gifts of love, needs a constancy of spirit.

As all the sins feed each other, Lust is fed by the cravings of Envy. We have said that Envy believes that everyone should be able to do and enjoy and experience whatever anyone else can do and enjoy and experience, and perhaps there are a few things after which we lust more today than the experiences that we have not so far enjoyed or endured. Since Lust will not take the time or trouble to explore or develop any relationship to the full, none can satisfy it; it will whip itself (perhaps an appropriate term in the context) to try anything that will revive its jaded feelings. It is tired of fellatio. Then it will try its hand (hardly the appropriate phrase in the context) at a little sodomy. Weary of only one partner, it will advance to group sex. Unsure at last of its own sexuality, it will have recourse to bisexuality. Wearied and bored by the flesh, it will call for chains and leather jackets. Who knows when, abandoning the last shred of its humanity, it will turn to bestiality? All of this is again often interpreted as proof that our age is more sexually active than any before, whereas it is evidence rather that the lustfulness of our time has reduced our sexuality almost to impotence.

Even in the more restrained workouts that are outlined in *The Joy of Sex*, we read instructions for those who live in a time in which the theme and fear of sexual impotence dominate our lives and much of our literature. Our sexuality has been animalized, stripped of the intricacy of feeling with which human beings have endowed it, leaving us to contemplate only the act, and to fear our impotence in it. It is this animalization from which the sexual manuals cannot escape, even when they try to do so, because they are reflections of it. They might be textbooks for veterinarians. All of this leads in the end to a dejection or slothfulness of feeling. What ought to be a mutual enchantment, something not on our minds but springing in our whole beings, is drained of its gladness.

To say that sex has been made humorless is to say more than may at first be apparent. Our humor toward each other is one of the most precious gifts of our humanity, and never should it play more delightfully than when we lie with each other, exposed and vulnerable, yet never more at ease than in the complete exchange of interest and familiarity. Such a play of humor is seldom to be found with a stranger, and never will it be found if stranger merely follows stranger to one's bed. It requires affection, familiarity, and unspoken confidence. This humor and playfulness have evaporated from Lust, and the sexual manuals make of sex a work ethic. Labor at it, they say.

Sexual parathesia is a term used by theology to denote various kinds of perversion, in which "sex life is not affected by venereal matters, but by objects altogether foreign to sex life": sadism and masochism, fetishism and homosexuality, the last of which is also condemned as the sin of sodomy. One does not have to agree with the Church in condemning homosexuality as a sin, to say that much of the attraction to it today seems to derive from something that we have already observed: the widespread disinclination to become involved, especially in what is intended to be a longstanding if not lifelong relationship in which the demands may be many and substantial. Homosexual relationships are *in general*, and generally by their nature, impermanent and do not make as many demands as a heterosexual relationship that exists in the context of raising a family. They inevitably bring into play fewer expressions of our personalities than do relationships with those of the other sex. Homosexuality carries with it some of the symptoms of Lust as it has been described here. Its relationships are not notably marked by the expectation of involvement or continuance, and there is especially not the involvement that is intended in sharing the task of raising a family. What is interesting about the word "gay" is that it celebrates a general lack of involvement as well as homosexuality as such.

But sadism, masochism, and fetishism are in a different realm, and the fascination with them today suggests that, just as they reflect a hideous emptiness in the individuals who practice them, they reflect a no less terrible emptiness in our societies. We have said that Lust is a form of self-emptying, but there has been an emptiness there already. In no other sin does one feel so much of a void, and this void is not only inside, it is also outside in the society. There is a profound failure of our societies to make continuing individual relationships seem part of the much wider social bonds that tie us to them. Marriage and family are still the basic units of our society, but they are weakened, and we tend to regard them today as a matter only of interpersonal relationships, rather than as fundamental elements of the social order. This changed attitude to marriage has resulted inevitably in a changed attitude to other personal relationships. Our fascination with various forms of sexual perversion is a direct result of the fact that our personal relationships now rest only on their own self-justification. It is not surprising that, in such a situation, when it is only our enjoyment that can please us, we say that "anything goes."

There is no more pat shibboleth of our time than the idea that what consenting adults do in private is solely their own business. This is false. What we do in private has repercussions on ourselves, and what we are and believe has repercussions on others. What we do in our own homes will inevitably affect, not only our own behavior outside them, but what we expect and tolerate in the behavior of others, and what we expect the rulers of our societies to tolerate. A change in manners or discipline in the family will not leave unchanged the manners and discipline in the wider society. If we blaspheme in private, we will blaspheme in public. It may not be for society to intervene and punish us for what we do in private—although it does interfere if two consenting adults are to be found mistreating their child in their own home—but the idea that what we do in private is not its concern is nonsense and dangerous.

Some of the evils to which theology says that Lust will give rise are: blindness of intellect in respect of divine things; precipitancy in acting without judgment; want of regard for what befits one's state or person; inconstancy in good; hatred of God as an Avenger of such sins; love of this world and its pleasures; inordinate fear of death. Even if we set aside those that are directly concerned with our relationship with God, we are still left with the fact that Lust, no less than the other sins, affects our conduct and attitudes to life in ways beyond its own immediate interests. When we remind ourselves how deeply our sexual feelings are registers of our whole beings, it is mere trifling to say that our societies ought not to be alert to the way in which we enjoy them. "Lust is a capital vice, because the carnal pleasure of which we are speaking is so attractive to the majority of mankind that man is led into all kinds of disorders, in order to gratify his fleshly desires." Which of us will deny it?

Our obsession with our sexuality has led us to develop a wholly false, rather silly, and in the end objectionable view of our natures. Our sexual life is taken to be the measure of our entire life. If we are what our age chooses to define as "sexually irresponsive," we are said to be "frigid" or at least abnormal. Elaine Morgan had the courage to write in the *New York Times* recently—so unusual was it to read such views these days it seemed like courage!—about what she called the "submerged minority" of those who are not particularly interested in sexual activity and may even (Lord have mercy upon us!) not be interested in it at all. "What few people [in these days] are gullible enough to believe in is virgins. Well, I believe in them," she said. "They are still around, among both sexes, and they are not all under the age of fourteen." She reminded us how many people in the past sublimated their sexual energies into works of considerable achievement of benefit to others as well as themselves. "Today we would not say that these energies had been sublimated; we would say that they have been inhibited. We have this arbitrary conviction that, if you have the biological capacity to do something and yet don't want to do it, then you are 'inhibiting' your deepest instincts, and this must be bad." She underlined her point: "There is no evidence that sex is a categorical imperative like food and oxygen; and there is no evidence that voluntary abstention from it leads to neurosis or emotional disturbance." The most telling thing about her article was the shock of reading it in the *New York Times* under the headline "In Defense of Virgins." So far have we come.

For the mark of her argument was its common sense. She welcomed the increased sexual tolerance in our age but merely asked that it should be extended to "both ends of the spectrum," to those who prefer not to engage in sexual activity as well as to those who wish to do so. It is this genuine tolerance and common sense that have been virtually ruled out by the sexual propaganda to which we are today subjected, and against which almost no one seems to dare to raise a voice out of fear of the retorts and even (as Elaine Morgan said) the hilarity that might be provoked. It is always in the power of propaganda to cause fear and anxiety in those at whom it is aimed, and it is fear and anxiety in those who are normal and balanced and even innocent that it causes in this case. There is something despicable and cheap, a demeaning of all real humanity, in the way in which this propaganda has been used.

One can only suppose that there is a cause for it all

beyond mere prurience and lack of caring. If our societies have good reason to be interested in our sexual attitudes and behavior, we have no less reason to be interested in why our societies have encouraged us to look to sex for such morbid delectation. The lustful person will usually be found to have a terrible hollowness at the center of his life, and he is agitated to fill it, not daring to desist, lest he should have to confront the desert he has made of himself and his life. He has no spiritual resource to which to turn. But is this not the condition of our societies as well? Moral theology has a pleasing and useful phrase: In the discussion of "non-consummated sins of impurity," Article I is addressed to "Sexual Commotion," which is defined as "the pleasurable disturbance or excitement of the genital organs and the fluids that serve the purpose of generation." (It assures us in passing that "it is best not to bother about *slight* and *quickly passing* carnal commotions," although "some positive resistance is generally necessary in case of vehement carnal commotion.") We seem these days to be in a continual state of commotion about our sex, and it is hard to resist the conclusion that this is partly because our societies themselves are in a commotion, that they have themselves no spiritual resources on which to call that enables either them or ourselves as individuals to be calm.

Our societies do not know why they are there, except to continue; we hardly know why we are members of them, except to survive. It is all but inevitable in such a condition, with nothing very much outside ourselves to hold our attention for long, that we should agitate the most easily aroused and placable of our physical and emotional urges, if only to reassure ourselves that we are still alive and sentient beings. When our societies assist in reducing most of the rest of life to little more than a series of disconnected episodes, commotions that only distract us, they cannot be surprised that their members reduce their own lives to a series of disconnected encounters, to find distraction in the everyday commotion of their sexual organs. Lust is always the symptom of a much deeper disorder, in society as in the individual, than the assuaging of its dreary appetite might at first suggest. Again there is something in the individual's relationship with society that is terribly awry.

We do not see how parched our social landscape has become, because it is studded with gaudy and erotogenic allurements to what we conceive to be a pleasure that is within the easy reach of us all. The managers of our societies much prefer that we are infatuated with our sexuality, than that we look long and steadily at what they contrive from day to day. They have little to fear as long as we define ourselves by the measurements of Masters and Johnson, and seem to find our most revolutionary tract in *The Joy of Sex*. They have discovered that, now that religion has been displaced, sex can be made the opium of the masses. When the entire society is at last tranquilly preoccupied in the morbid practices of onanism, there will be nothing more for them to do but reign forever over a kingdom of the dead.

It is worth leaving the last of the sins with Dante as he leaves the last cornice of the Blessed Mountain, where the lustful have been purged, to enter at last the meadows of the Earthly Paradise, with the benediction of the Angel of Chastity singing in his ears: *Beati mundo corde:* blessed are the pure in heart—"a sound/more than all earthly music sweet and ringing." And again the glad angel sings *Venite benedicti patri:* "Come ye blessed, inherit the kingdom prepared for you from the foundation of the world." When the seventh and last stair has been climbed, Virgil sends him forward on his own, "Make pleasure now thy guide." Since the stain of sin has been purged and love has been set again in order, the aid of human reason is necessary no more and his own pleasure can be trusted. Love itself has become what it ought always to have been, the only needful guide to right conduct. "Love, and do as you like" as St. Augustine said, because, so loving, we will do what we ought.

Virgil points in farewell to the meadows that lie before them and leaves Dante with the last promise that soon he will set his eyes on Beatrice again:

> See how the sun shines here upon thy head;
>> See the green sward, the flowers, the boskages
>> That from the soil's own virtue here are bred.
>
> While those fair eyes are coming, bright with bliss,
>> Whose tears sent me to thee, thou may'st prospect
>> At large, or sit at ease to view all this.
>
> No word from me, no futher sign expect;
>> Free, upright, whole, thy will henceforth lays down
>> Guidance that it were error to neglect,
>
> Whence o'er thyself I mitre thee and crown.

The soul has been purified in its long ascent, and, having now mastery of itself, being "free, upright, whole," Virgil invests it with the symbols of earthly power. Who does not catch his breath at this moment?

The penance of the lustful has been fire. It is the only time that the traditional "Purgatory Fire" is found in the poem, but now as Dorothy Sayers says, the image blazes out with a sudden splendid lucidity. Fire is the image of Lust, but it is also the image of Purity. Love must endure again the flames of its own passion, but it is also the flame of love that burns to purge it. In this tremendous image at the moment of the triumphant ascent, Dante proclaims again the truth to which the idea of sin draws attention: that love is at the root of both our virtue and our evil. As the lustful run round the Blessed Mountain in opposite directions, they embrace one another swiftly as they pass, "not pausing, with this brief salute content," and their kiss is again the image both of their sinning and of its remedy. The power of this accumlated imagery is not easily resisted. Even those who, although detained on the seventh cornice, are not detained to purge the sin of lust, must still pass through its fire. Since every sin is a sin of love, misdirected or perverted, the love in each of us must itself be purged. It is with this affirmation that the ascent of purgatory is brought to an end, and the meaning of our sinning stands forth with all its complexity and searching, and with a pointing to hope and life.

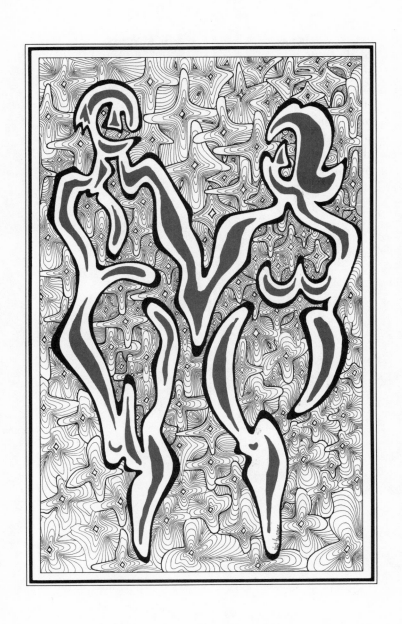

THE PATHS OF LOVE

THE PATHS OF LOVE

SIN IS NOT just lovelessness, the absence of love. Its terribleness is that love has been present, only to be rejected; even more bleakly, love is the raw material on which sin works. Sin is the wreckage of the love of which we are capable. To acknowledge it in ourselves is to recognize what loving creatures we might have been, to realize how pitifully we diminish our capacity to love. Everyone who loves knows how inadequate his love is, how his own selfish wants get in the way. Every soul that Dante meets in purgatory has come to this knowledge, mourning what it has made of its life, sorrowing that it should have so misused God's gift of love to it. They may have to endure the penance of each sin—the heavy stones of Pride, the sealed eyes of Envy, the smoke of Anger, the running of Sloth, the prostration of Avarice, the starvation of Gluttony, the fire of Lust—but the scourge of each sin consists of examples of the opposing virtues, and each of them—humility, generosity, meekness, zeal, liberality, temperance, chastity—is an example of love that is in order.

A great part of our living must be the attempt to put our own love in order. In terms that are as concrete as possible, and at the risk of simplifying its character, we must consider love in some of its aspects. Few things could have been more misleading than the way in which the flower children and their like spoke of love a few years ago. They seemed to think that love is a matter of no more than demonstrating one's own feelings. For all the apparent sweetness of their offerings, there was in fact a great deal of self-aggrandizement in it. I love you; my love will bless you; be thankful for it; see how loving I am. Even when they greeted strangers on the streets, forcing the strangers into attitudes of rejection, they turned away with a simpering look of superiority. The strangers were uptight; but they of course were loving. It never occurred to them that the strangers merely distrusted such indiscriminate and meaningless approaches and reserved the right to choose by whose love they would be blessed and on whom they would bestow their own. Yet these young people were often encouraged in their simplemindedness by their elders, until one began to believe that the love shown in their homes had also been false.

One addressed audiences of students at the time and said love was difficult. In the language of their love, "Bullshit! Bullshit!" came the reply. One said that love could easily be selfish, that certainly it could be misdirected or distorted, and that then it could threaten and wound. "Make Love Not War" was the message on their buttons; then let them know that a too-easy love can hurt as well. They stirred still protesting in their seats; they did not wish to be told such things. Yet all one was saying was that love can be disordered, a fact that all human experience and much of our literature seems to confirm; that it may spring from the wrong motives and be directed in wrong ways to its object, that it can indeed be the source of our evil as well as of our virtue. We are entitled to take these young as representative of more general attitudes that are still around us, because once again they seemed to have learned little of the nature of love from their background: nothing of its complexity, from parents or teachers, literature or religion. There was simply this love, freely given, and all would be harmony. The idea of the "war of the sexes," beside this flummery, has at least some hard truth in it.

The essential quality of human love is its incorrigible

ambition to transcend whatever is its immediate object. There are not two lovers who do not believe that their love will conquer time—not merely time here, but even the grave—and the wonder is that we still prefer to leave unanswered the question whether it can. When the lovers in Auden's ballad, "When I Went Out One Evening," protest their undying love for each other, all the clocks in the city begin to whir, with their message that love cannot conquer time, but when the clocks go silent again, and the lovers have left, the river runs on, and the question still hangs in the air. Even in this most common of cases, the belief that there is something transcendent in human love is there, telling us of its nature as we perceive it, of the power of which we are aware when this deepest of our feelings is aroused, so that the world itself can seem changed.

When our eyes fall with love on some person or object, they then turn out to find more in the world that deserves our fondness, and that we are able to love better than before. When we have first taken the trouble to learn how really to love a painting, we do not then sit in front of it alone for the rest of our lives. Our ability to love one painting has opened an entire new world to us, which we are now able to enter with the capacity to discriminate and love others. This is again a form of transcendence. If it truly is love, it extends our lives and widens our vision, the world is not the same. Lovers are not only interesting to themselves; everything is more interesting to them. We think of the truest marriages that we know as partnerships. The mutual fondness and support is used to turn their lives out, to act upon a world that is other than themselves and invite it to act upon them. All true love has some object other than itself and can point to some achievement beyond its own existence. Love cannot be the only source and intimation of its own reality and cannot keep in touch with the rest of reality by admiring itself.

Love is not a matter of looking into each other's eyes, it has been said, but of looking in the same direction. Of course it is both. But the look with which it should be turned out needs to be emphasized. If all love is a journey into another land, it will to some extent be a land that it itself creates and then cultivates and even peoples, but it will also be a land that has its own existence and that love does not make a reflection of itself, just as it does not find a mere reflection in the person it loves. The lovers will together be turned out to the substantial world that lies beyond the circumference of their own feelings for each other. If lovers look at the stars, their instinct is right. They are looking outward for the full meaning, as they should also look out together to their society. Their love will otherwise be only another form of self-love. They will have made even it narcissistic, and it will perish.

We start our lives with what is often given the name of need-love. But the term has its disadvantages. It can suggest too passive a relationship, in which the person who is loved is used merely to supply one's wants, and it emphasizes too much the element of dependence. Of course, there are need and dependence when the infant wants to be fed and when out of fear or frustration or hurt a child runs to its mother for protection and comfort. But as infancy passes into childhood, the relationship grows more complex. The child will still rely on its parent, but not simply to supply the needs that it feels. The mother may in fact refuse to meet the child's needs to the extent it would like, believing that in some situations the child must itself cope with its fears and hurts. And the parent also begins to rely on the child for some things. The relationship is not equal, but at least it is two-sided. Dependent or need-love is giving way to what we may call *reliant love*.

Reliant love does not just seek love, it is a way of giving

love as well, because it grants the other an active role, the freedom to choose how to love in return. The infant who wants food or warmth, or merely to be held by its mother, has only to be supplied with these, and it will coo in return. The mother may take pleasure in it, but the infant does not yet give pleasure. This comes only as it crosses from infancy into childhood, when the relationship is perhaps most crucial, for the child who is then nourished to feel reliant rather than dependent love will know how to feel it later. Dependent love in the adult is weak and will make the other weak. Reliant love can be strong and make the other strong. In reliant love one asks to be not so much assuaged as known; one seeks less a reaction from than an interaction with someone else. One's felt needs can be an expression of the merest self-indulgence and may well not reflect one's real needs at all. Therefore one does not ask that they be met simply because one feels them; one asks rather to express the whole of one's personality to someone who is other and distinct and who brings his or her own insights and even needs into play against one's own.

It is important to emphasize this at the beginning. There is a great deal of confusion today about the role of dependence in love, about the kind of needs we are entitled to bring to a relationship, and how far and in what ways we may expect that relationship to supply them. In the absence of any strong concept of love, the prescriptions are little more, as we have seen, than for massage and manipulation, which are usually the reverse sides of the same coin. One comes to a relationship with needs before one comes with anything else, and they will be massaged or manipulated. (It does not much matter which, for if there is open aggression in the manipulation, in the massage there is the guile of what is known to psychiatry as passive aggression.) What is always absent is even the possibility that two people may trust each other to place on their relationship an equal value for their own sakes and even for its own sake—for what they have made has its own worth—and it is hard to resist the impression that the prescriptions are made for and by people who were not nourished in their childhood to cross from need-love to reliant love. Their love is that of infants.

It is need nonetheless that largely determines the child's relationships, not only with its parents but with others whom it selects to love. This is true even of friends of its own age, for most of the friendships of school and childhood are alliances. They are formed against an unknown and threatening world. There is nothing wrong with such alliances then, or with reliant love as one element in a relationship later. But no sooner has the child learned that reliant love is not the old need-love, when all its wants were met apparently on demand, than a new feeling begins to stir in it with the first arousals of puberty. For it is not only sex that rouses it; and it is perhaps not even primarily sex. In fact there is considerable evidence that, if left to itself, early adolescence may be a time of sexual interest but not of a pressing need for much activity. What present themselves are rather the intimations of what used to be known as first love. The importance of first love was that it was a first tentative and wondering, ecstatic and painful, brave and adventuring, shared exploration of someone whom one had chosen oneself out of nothing but one's own love. Reliance is hardly a part of such love, for one knows little on which to rely. One is not needing or depending; one is risking and daring. Reliant love has been overtaken by the first calls to what may be described as *bestowing love*. One bestows all one has and is on someone else. One crowns them. Adults will look on with the knowing of their years, but if they are truly wise they will be silent, and let the voyagers go forward with the prayer, "Be happy, be hurt," and be there to catch the tears.

We sometimes seem to have bred a generation—and many of their number agree—that has never known the explorations of first love. They are already so worldly wise, even as they enter their teens, unable to believe the improbable or dream the impossible, unwilling to try and risk, afraid to get involved with all their feelings. Yet there is much in first love that teaches of loving. There is usually an awkwardness in its first sexual approaches—or rather not an awkwardness, since it is attractive—but at least a fumbling with no sexual manual for instruction. The wondering young lovers do not grope merely to find out how to perform what is, by any reckoning, a rather eccentric act of coupling if viewed objectively, but to discover how they may tell, through their bodies as they have not known them before, the sweep of their new feelings for each other, which they have not known for anyone else. Even their first "forevers," although they will be disappointed, do not in the end deceive. What they meant by that "forever" will remain in their lives, as will the sense of discovery of another being whom they later turn to love.

It is also one of the virtues of first love that it introduces one to the pain of rejection. It savors even the heartbreaks. There is a peculiar quality in the breaking up of a first love. There may be a great deal of misery; there is rarely much accusation. The rejected one may pine, ask plaintively if this had not been "the flower of the ages, and the first love of the world," as of course it had been, sob that it had been meant forever, cry that life (even so early!) has lost its meaning. But he or she does not much blame. It is almost as if the unhappiness is too great for accusation. A fine discrimination is being made. There is a world of difference between pain and sorrow. Pain is turned in to feel for oneself; sorrow is still turned out to the other, even though the other is now lost. Those whose pain at the ending of a love is greater than their sorrow have not truly loved. Hearts *can* be broken. And perhaps what we mean by a broken heart is not only the all-but-unbearable sorrow at losing the presence of someone much loved, but a slight tightening of the heart against risking any further disappointment. The danger to a broken heart is a fear that the world in the end has no place for what is especially lovely and that time will inexorably wear away even the brightest promise of any love in its beginning. First love helps one to build a guard against such disillusion. Sighing for a loveliness that still exists, sorrowing at the loss of what has not lost its beauty, the heart mends with its own love in good order. Those who have abandoned themselves to first love seem later to have a great emotional resource.

Some will say that this is a romantic description of first love and perhaps also by implication of any love between a man and a woman. Maybe, but it is rooted where all true romanticism is rooted, in reality. Romanticism must be ready to confront reality from day to day. It cannot afford to turn aside from the encounter, neither to disillusion nor to sentimentality. Such victories as romanticism can ever claim are wrung from a bedrock of reality, from the hard and ungiving facts of what is actually so in the world and in life. What is important in first love is not that it is sweet and charming, but that it is a first exploration of reality that is made essentially by oneself, even it if is made also in the company of someone else whom one has chosen to share it. One may go to extremes, fall head over heels in love, give all that one has— only to find in the end, the most crushing of lessons, that one's giving is not enough. First love has run up against the limits of bestowing love! All of adolescence is this first exploration of reality by oneself, of one's own limits, and of the boundaries of the actual world, and first love can be among the most telling of its encounters. But our societies and their culture have blighted both adolescence and first love. They have instructed the young to learn too early and from others what they should discover in their own time by themselves, finding in their rapture and first intimations of sorrow that life is infinitely forgiving to those who meet it without fear.

If adolescence includes the exploration of first love, it also includes the first real exploration of friendship. It is at college or when one goes to work that one feels for the first time that one truly chooses one's own friends and even thinks seriously of the possibility that friendships are meant to last for a lifetime. They are not allies found in the area defined by one's school and one's parents' home. One also finds something else: that "friendship is an education in complexity," as Hilaire Belloc once wrote to a friend of a mutual friend, who at the time was being difficult to them both. Friendship is not the only, and certainly not the greatest, love that is unpossessive. But that it is unpossessive is the most obvious of its characteristics. There are no ties or vows or promises that bind it, and yet sometimes its bonds seem stronger than any others. A friend may uproot his life and go to Timbuktu, without so much as a by one's leave, and it is wholly in his right to do so. Yet even across the distance he remains one's friend. He may behave as one did not expect him to do, perhaps cause one bewilderment and even pain, but still one will know him as one's friend. This is indeed an education in complexity.

With friendship one is introduced to *disinterested love*. For what is a friend meant to give one? Nothing really, except himself. Friends drop out of one's life and then drop back in again, unbidden and unannounced, and still they are welcome. Friends come early and stay late; or they come late and stay to make up for it. Friends are frequently outrageous in their behavior, relying on one to understand when a mere acquaintance would not; and they are in fact often more outrageous than we notice, simply because we do not question their conduct or see it as a slight. Friends do not think of forgiving each other.

They do not ask each other to change. If they happen to quarrel, they have few questions to put and none that calls for explanation or justification. They only want to enjoy again what delights them, not only in each other, but in the uniqueness of the company they make.

The English philosopher Michael Oakeshott has said that one may leave one's butcher for another if he gives one bad meat, one's tailor for another if he makes one an ill-fitting suit, but one does not replace a friend by another just because he turns out to be not altogether what one thought and does not give one all that one wants or has been used to receiving. We may be fortunate to find new friends over the years, but no new friend can take the place of another. What we ask from friends is not a service, but the opportunity to enjoy each of them as they are, and to enjoy oneself with them as with no one else, not even with another friend who also is irreplaceable. Even in absence over time and distance, the friends may change, but their apprehension of each other does not. After a long separation they pick up where they had left off, almost as if it were yesterday. The importance of this love cannot be overestimated. One's capacity for it will inform every other love. It is possible to form a great friendship with someone of the opposite sex, without romantic attachment or sexual exchange; not only can such a friendship be as rewarding as any, but the person who is incapable of it will be a poor lover of any individual member of the opposite sex. And equally, the woman who is capable of real friendship with women will also be a better friend of men, and vice versa.

But friends are to turn to, it will be said; they are for support and advice, help and reassurance. One can call on a friend. All of which is true in a way, and yet not exactly true, for this is not *why* he or she is a friend. There is no obligation in friendship, so if he is not there when one needs him, the friendship will not be altered. He is likely to be there if he can, but that is not the test of the friendship. When one of them needs help or advice, two friends will meet, discuss the difficulty, decide what should and may be done, and then push it aside, the helper and the helped, to get back to what their friendship really means to them, their mutual enjoyment in it and in each other. There is an endless curiosity in friendship, and this is perhaps the root of its love. One simply wants to know what he is up to now, where he thinks he is going next, and why he has taken to standing on his head. Friendship is anecdote. The best of anecdotes are told by friends about friends: They spring from a delighting observation of the other. What is enjoyed in friendship is the narrative of someone else's life, in which one shares to some extent, but lived as he or she chooses to live it to his or her own ends. As a friend one is not so much in the other's life as alongside it, and there one stays even when apart.

Each of these is an ordinary form of human love as we learn to express and receive it in our everyday lives. Each has its virtues. None of them, especially in the adult, is complete in itself. Reliant love by itself is love half-grown. In spite of all its enchantments and its readiness to give everything it has, bestowing love by itself is too heedless of the real character of the other; it ought to make a demand on the other to be credible, and to lift the suspicion that it is not "in love with love" and with its own ability to love. Friendship by itself is committed, perhaps as much as any other form of love, but what is its strength is also its limitation, that it is not closely involved from day to day. The three need to collaborate, to check and enhance each other. When one finds them combined in a relationship, and the powerful impetus of sexual pleasure is added, one is close to the mature love between a man and woman, which grows and flourishes even in difficulty. Let the reliance grow too routine, the bestowing will be there with its gifts; let the bestowing grow slack for a while, the reliance will hold the ground; let one of them be out of love or simply out of sorts, friendship is there with the patience of its appreciativeness.

When the young person is first introduced to them and has been nourished to respond to their promptings, what he and she are feeling is the pull of their moral natures and the need to give them expression: their need to turn out and be committed to what is not themselves; their need to be loyal to someone or even something that is other. The young would not go on trying from generation to generation, in spite of all that human experience has to tell, if the urge was not deep and awakening and irresistible. We may see evidence of this around us today. After all the tawdry experiments in human relationships a decade ago, there is a significant number among the young responding again to the need for commitment, with the understanding that this commitment must essentially be that of one person to a second individual. They have realized that, without this expression of their natures, they do not know themselves. We said at the beginning that sin is betrayal, just as the most obvious quality of love is loyalty. But it is a betrayal not only of others but of oneself, a refusal to be loyal to even the deepest part of one's own being.

We have all but abandoned the big words to talk of the big things. Loyalty—Comradeship—Patriotism—Fidelity: We wince when we try to utter them. They die on our lips. Which of us now thinks of Glory in his life, strives for or even thinks to attain it? Bravery and Cowardice: Do we any longer know the difference? We praise the deserter, and disdain the comrade, at least until we look closer. For the trouble with the deserter is that, even as one applauds him for defecting in a good cause, he will usually then be found ready to defect in a bad one, and not least to desert oneself at his whim; whereas the truth about the comrade is that, although one may wonder about his loyalty to a bad cause, he will be found to remain loyal to whatever cause he embraces and not least to prove his comradeship with oneself. "Loyalty?" Harold Macmillan once said in answer to a question. "Loyalty? . . . It is knowing that the man on your left, and the man on your right, will not let you down." It was an image from the trenches of World War I, but also from a generation that knew what comradeship is, set great store by it, and had a strong word for it in its vocabulary, because it had meaning.

What has been taken from us is the ability to set an unconditional value on things or people other than ourselves: to say that for these at least, to put it at the extreme, we would lay down our lives. Even if there were no people or things that actually have such a value, we are bound as human beings to give an absolute worth to something. We need the ideal; we need it to inspire and correct us; we need it to praise. Most of the big words are words of praise of the ideal or of our refusal of it. But our culture will not speak to us of the ideal or even admit that something worthwhile is being denied, and so it is unable to teach us how to praise. When was the last time that a novel, a play, or a movie showed us an ideal friendship, rooted in the heart, in the capacity for loyalty, and in the longing to admire what we love? When indeed was the last time that it showed us our ideal selves, which we are unable to be, but held before us as a lamp of what we still may strive to be? What else is our humanity but this striving, the awareness of our backsliding, but then with the heart and will renewed to try again? The human race sometimes seems to have a peculiar way of advancing. It falteringly takes one step forward, then slips two back, but does not quite lose all the ground. The ground has been occupied by our vocabulary. We leave our words there to hold it, representations of where we yet may go, and may hope someday at last to be. But something has seeped into our societies that belittles these ideal representations, and we are more at a loss without them than we know.

The religious would say that it is our rejection of God, and their case is not easily met or dismissed. Does it not seem that, since the "death of God," man has himself become a black hole, collapsing into himself? But those of us who are unbelievers may still point to something more immediate. Our societies have systematically undermined our consciences, the place where our ideal selves are rooted and admonish us. There is not one of us who does not feel the bidding of conscience, know that it is a commanding voice in us to be obeyed or disobeyed at risk, and yet find ourselves deafened to it by voices that tell us that we may painlessly disregard it. Call the conscience the superego, if one will, or merely the warning voice of the superego, it does not matter. There it sits; there it stands. In terms more traditional, it tells us how to be human, and so how to be ourselves. The destruction of this humanness is the work of our societies. If we disregard our consciences and listen instead to false prophets, it is our societies that have raised them, so many and to such prominence, not only in the marketplace where we might expect them but in the most sacred of our groves.

Even our capacity for self-love is corrupted. Those who love themselves well—as we need and ought to do— will regard what they love as gifts to them. It would be simplest to say that we love what is good in ourselves because it is a gift from God. But even if we do not believe that there is a God who works in us in this way, we can still acknowledge that what we rightly love in ourselves, what we most love ourselves for, is at least partly owed to the working of others in our lives: not only of our parents and teachers and friends and neighbors, not only of those bonds to our society that broaden our sense of ourselves, but the working also of our faulty but striving civilization, even of what we call the folk memory of the human race down the eons. To love ourselves well is partly to love these in us, what we have made of them and they of us. But our societies have more and more severed our sense of them. Not only have they withered our capacity to love. They have left us little to love at all.

We cannot hope to love our world today if we do not make the attempt to love it through our science. Modern science has radically altered how we both experience and perceive reality. It therefore alters in turn our sense of ourselves and our values. We look too much to our art to-day for our perceptions and too little to the revelations of our science. What does it mean to us individually that we may be a not very spectacular star in a not very impressive galaxy, only one star among billions in one galaxy among millions, our own galaxy some 100,000 light years in diameter, other galaxies more than 10 billion light years away? What does it mean to us when we gaze into the no less astonishing submicroscopic world with its marvelously organized arrangement of rank upon rank of things so minute that they are no more easily imagined than the great distances of space that stretch beyond us?

It is not only that we know different things than before about the universe, and therefore of our place in it; about our environment, and therefore of how we move about and interact with it. Our ideas of what we can know, and how we may know it, of our opportunities and our limitations, have also altered. What does it mean to us that our science no longer presents to us a world of fixed laws as in a piece of clockwork, but laws only of probability and chance that at least seem to conform to what we at present believe we are able to explain? What does it mean to us that our science is no longer just the observer and recorder of what is taken to be reality but is now active as a participator in its own observations and experiments by which it defines that reality? What does it mean that our science now moves backward and forward between the theoretical models that it builds and the practical experiments to which it then subjects them, so that the experiment is continually altering the model and the model in turn is continually redefining the experiment? What does it mean when so much of our science has to be communicated in its own language, whose symbols are untranslatable into those which we use in daily life? What is it that we know when we say we know?

What does it mean to us when the inquiries of science are now so involved in what used to be the concerns of philosophy—the nature of time and space and matter—and when they make use of so many disciplines that it previously held aloof from it? What does it mean that our view of the universe takes on some of the characteristics even of history, since we do not now observe an immutable creation but cosmic events that occurred in time and will not happen again? What does it mean that, bereft of our science, we would no longer know how to look? What does it mean that so awesome a universe is revealed to us by a method that tells us no less awesomely of the reach of the human mind, and that we live at the brink of knowing still so much more?

It means that we should learn to love the creation of which we are part even more than before, to praise even more wonderingly the amazing complexity and beauty that we are being shown, to marvel with even more gravity, but also joy, at the still incomprehensible phenomenon of our own place in it, to know that this above all is of unconditional value and worth every effort of knowing and understanding. If we look small against the backdrop of the universe, little more than spin-offs from the laws of chance as they have worked, we are not small in our endeavor to scan the whole universe, the strongest of our motives simply to know it from every viewpoint in which we can place ourselves. Even if it means taking ourselves out of the center of the universe, making ourselves seem adrift in both time and space, we do not halt our effort or bury our knowledge. In nothing has our science made us more free than in the fearlessness of its search for truth and its willingness to confront it.

There is something else to which we do not attend enough, even though it could hardly be more important and even surprising. There is now in our science itself a transcending of ourselves that could not be more firmly grounded in reality, for it lies in our own attempts to understand the reality by which we are surrounded from day to day. It forces us to recognize our limits but then pushes us beyond them, to contemplate as never before the vastness, the complexity, and the endurance of the creation of which we are part, and the extent of our own reach into it. But not only these. Modern science has presented us with a picture of creation that has an unutterable beauty. Even literally, its pictures are exquisite, whether they are of some distant star or of the smallest particle that it can represent. There is no need to add fiction to this science. We can see our universe and our world, and the creatures in it, as only our century has had the chance. We can see it, we can feel it. The infinite richness of the texture of all that forms creation is more at our fingertips than ever in the past. At no time before has our science so obviously touched and enriched our aesthetic sense. At no time before has it come so near to appealing from its own illuminations to our religious sense. More than anything that is now available to us, it can help to take us out of ourselves. If we do not learn how to love this well, we will love less well ourselves and others.

At the very moment at which science has freed itself from too deterministic and rational a picture of the world, we seem unwilling to make the effort to bring it persistently to bear on our senses and values. We will not use its vision. There is perhaps no deeper reason for our egocentric and stunted image of ourselves. We prefer the trifling of an art and literature that arrogantly refuse the intimations that science could bring them and that prefer to celebrate only themselves and not the wonder of creation and life. When we turn to religion it is again to forms that have turned their backs on the reality that our science has revealed so intricately. We cannot hope to set our love in order, to be freed again to love others and ourselves as we should, if we do not trouble to love the world in which we live. For if one thing is clear, it is that our human loves need, if they are to be strong, some sense of meaning in the universe in which they are enacted.

To love others for their own sakes is not to love them only for themselves. If that were the case, it would be too easy to love them only for what they have to give, for the reward, so that one loves only one's own needs, which they supply. They must be loved as people who express to us in their own ways the goodness of all created things; this is the only way in which we can be sure that we love them standing apart from us in a world that is securely theirs; they are not just there for the taking because their own selves are rooted in their own relationship to what is real, lasting, and beyond them. Cannot we just love someone because we love that person? The answer is yes—but not entirely. We should not have to be reminded that love can be treacherous; even when it is not treacherous it will from time to time be clumsy. Our love needs correction and protection. The most complete love must be an expression of our care for the preciousness of another being. But if this precious otherness is to be left intact, it must be allowed its own setting in a world with which we cannot willfully interfere; the other must be loved among what also is other.

The love of a man and woman must be informed by a love also of others. This is what distinguishes it from all other forms of love. Reliant love does not seek to extend itself to others. Bestowing love has no interest in others. Friendship is curious about others but takes its main pleasure in itself. This is not the case of the love of man and woman, and it is what makes it unique and so challenging. What seems to be the most self-sufficient love is most needing of resources outside itself. The loved one cannot be isolated but must be loved as an existence that has its own life among other existences and draws some of its own liveliness and worth from them. Our gaze will turn constantly from the beloved to the other human beings who are around us from day to day, and from them back to the beloved, so that each enrichens the other, and not least ourselves and the shared love which then expands. Our central attachment to the person whom we have singled out becomes the center itself of an ever-widening circle of human relations, in which the personality of the other is brought fully into play and then is turned back to us with even more to offer and of which to tell. We have only to think of this outturned relationship in the most obvious of its expressions. Two go out in the evening and one notices the other across the room, expressing herself in ways different from those which she uses to him, and his appreciation of her manifoldness is only deepened and more delighted. When they return home, their gossip of the evening is full, as they talk as with no one else. Always this most intimate of relationships is embedded in social relationships that constantly give it much of its reinforcement and refreshment.

If our personal relationships today cause us so much anxiety, it is partly because our social relationships have become so pathetically attentuated. We demand satisfactions of our personal relationships that not even the strongest can be sensibly expected to supply, and ask of our societies only that they should reinforce us still further in our personal lives, where we whimper our discontents. Self is locked only with self. It is not only our most immediate social relationships that need to be strengthened; we must bring back our societies to the center of our personal lives. The love that is not ultimately informed by a concern for the wider society, for the endurance of our civilization, for the long tra ail of the human race, and at last for the unknowable wonder and mystery of the created universe, will itself turn into only another form of egocentricity that is bolstered by someone else. One cannot emphasize too often, since the mores of our time are all against it, that the unique quality of the love of man and woman, since they share their lives so fully, is that it reaches far beyond itself, in even the most ordinary of its daily rounds.

In the days before affluence was widespread, we could not turn our backs on our societies, perhaps especially in this relationship. Too much depended not only on the employment of the husband but on the housekeeping of the wife, and even on the work of the children. Through all of them the daily needs of the home extended it into a series of intricate relationships with relatives and neighbors. The family was always going out into the society; the society was always coming to the door. There was no way of imagining that what happened in the wider society did not touch one's own life, and there was no way of deceiving oneself that people should be judged by their inner feelings and not by their overt acts. What our affluent societies have done is break the ties of material necessity, without replacing them by others that compel us to take responsibility for ourselves and for others as social beings.

It is all very well to say with Robert J. Henle, a Jesuit, that "structures cannot be truly sinful," that "sin lies in the human will, and not in anything outside the soul," and to quote the reply of St. Francis Borgia, to a Spanish nobleman who was lamenting the corruption of the times: "I have a plan of reform. *I* will reform myself, and then *you* reform yourself, and so on." Well, yes! Of course! We need to reform ourselves and not be misled by the recipes for "self-improvement." But even if our societies were rich in "the more virtuous men and women" who are held out as their only hope, what evidence is there in the whole of history and in the world now that they would gain authority? We cannot wait for the improvement of our societies on the redemption of ourselves. Just as there is sin in us before we perform any sinful acts, so there is an inclination to injustice in our societies before they perform their unjust deeds.

The retreat into ourselves has blinded us to this fact, and that is why our societies are content to encourage it. The activity of the moral imagination that is now needed is to reacquire the understanding that, in ourselves and in the relationships that can all too easily become little more than extensions of ourselves, only a fraction of our whole natures is brought into play and given expression. It is our longing and our capacity to extend the working of our love—so that we can see it operating in our societies and strengthening our allegiance to them— against which we sin today more recklessly than ever before. Whichever way we turn for the remedy, we will find our sin in combat with our love. We will find our Pride, our Envy, our Anger, our Sloth, our Avarice, our Gluttony, and of course our Lust, at war with our human yearning to love the other children of our common birth. Since our societies have in effect surrendered any pretense to virtue, they are content that we should abandon any claim to it as well. They have no need for our virtue, since they can get along by manipulating our disposition to sin, and we acquiesce in this demeaning. Yet all the time there lies largely untapped in us the wanting of our natures to love what will not necessarily bring any other gratification. What that reaching out will bring is the blessing of feeling whole and alive to the world again. The paths of our loves will once more cross each other, converging and diverging, as they lead us out of ourselves: in directions of which we would not otherwise have thought, to encounters of which we now do not dream.

A CHECKLIST OF
SOME BOOKS

BEFORE THE GREAT Christian theologians was Aristotle. *The Nicomachean Ethics* cannot be ignored. It is available in several editions, but perhaps the best translation that is most accessible to the general reader is *The Ethics of Aristotle,* translated by J.A.K. Thomson (Penguin Books).

St. Thomas Aquinas should be read, and St. Jerome and St. Ambrose, but the great theologian on this subject is of course St. Augustine. *The City of God* is available as a Modern Library Giant, but once again Penguin has done a remarkable job in producing it as a one-volume paperback. As is said in the text, on the subject of sin his *Confessions* are vital reading. There are so many translations and editions available that there is no need to pick one out. If one really wishes to feel the anguish caused by sin and the wrestling against it, there is of course the sublime work of St. John of the Cross, *The Dark Night of the Soul,* translated by Kurt F. Reinhardt (Frederick Ungar).

The Divine Comedy of Dante is of course a key work, especially the second book *Purgatory.* It has never been translated altogether satisfactorily, but Dorothy L. Sayers's translation (Penguin) is more than adequate, and her introductions to the three volumes and her elaborate notes are just what most readers need.

The Ethics of Spinoza has been edited by Dagobert D. Runes and is published by Citadel Press.

For an exposition of the sins in moral theology, I found most useful the four volumes of Henry Davis, S.J.'s, *Moral and Pastoral Theology* (Sheed and Ward). But no recent work was more stimulating, as I began to think of this book, than *A Catalogue of Sins* by William F. May, and my obligation to it extends much farther than the few quotations in the text. It is interesting also as the work of a Protestant theologian. There are also E.J. Bicknell's *The Christian Idea of Sin and Original Sin in the Light of Modern Knowledge* (Longman, Green & Co.), Noel Hall's *The Seven Root Sins* (Oxford University Press), and E. Las B. Cherbonnier's *Hardness of Heart: A Contemporary Interpretation of the Doctrine of Sin* (Doubleday). But everyone can find his own favorites.

No one who writes on the subject can withhold a word of gratitude and admiration for Dorothy Sayers's lecture, *The Other Six Deadly Sins* (Methuen). There have been other books that have simply been part of my general reading over the years, of which I will mention only *The Devil's Share* by Denis de Rougement, which perhaps only a Frenchman could have written. To those who wish to enter the philosophical aspects of the subject, as they are debated today, one can highly recommend *Ethics and Christianity* by Keith Ward (George Allen & Unwin), and a tough little book, *A Defence of Theological Ethics* by G.F.Woods (Cambridge University Press).

I deliberately did not read *Whatever Happened to Sin?* by Karl Menninger (Hawthorn) before I finished my own manuscript, because it seemed better not to be influenced by what I knew to be a powerful argument from a distinguished clinical psychiatrist. I read it afterwards—he in fact courteously sent me an inscribed copy after my own essays had appeared in serial form—and I found it compelling. But since we approach the subject from angles so different, our books complement (rather than echo) each other.

I would add only one last work. Everyone should still read John Bunyan's *Pilgrim's Progress.*